Basic

Complete Communication

James Bury   **Anthony Sellick**   **Kaori Horiuchi**

JN062921

BOOK
1

SEIBIDO

photographs by
iStockphoto

音声ファイルのダウンロード／ストリーミング

CD マーク表示がある箇所は、音声を弊社 HP より無料でダウンロード／ストリーミングすることができます。下記 URL の書籍詳細ページに音声ダウンロードアイコンがございますのでそちらから自習用音声としてご活用ください。

http://seibido.co.jp/ad634

Complete Communication Book 1 – Basic –

PREFACE

In today's global society it is becoming increasingly important to be able to communicate in a wide range of contexts. This includes talking and writing about different topics, interacting with different people, and building knowledge of vocabulary in order to express opinions and justify them.

Complete Communication is a new series of textbooks that aims to develop students' overall communication skills, incorporating both receptive and productive activities. *Complete Communication Book 1 – Basic –* is the first book in the series.

Each of the fifteen units in the *Complete Communication Book 1 – Basic –* student book looks at a specific topic that people will encounter regularly, whether in everyday conversations or in more formal situations, such as examinations. The topics range from hometowns and family to shopping and plans.

Each unit follows a set plan and incorporates easy to follow activities. There are opportunities to learn and practice vocabulary in each unit as well as activities that focus on the gist and the details of listening texts. Each unit also incorporates three speaking activities that can be used in a controlled manner and sections which help with pronunciation and grammar. Each unit is also accompanied by two activities in the appendix that encourage further extended speaking and writing.

In addition to helping build students' knowledge of communicative English by providing practice for the core language needed to interact effectively in pair conversations and small group discussions, this series has been developed to enhance students' self-perceptions of ability and levels of confidence when using English. By doing this, it is hoped that students will come to see learning English as fulfilling, engaging, and fun, and that English is a language of communication and interaction in real-world situations, not just a language to be studied for tests.

We hope that you will find the topics and activities interesting and thought-provoking, and that they encourage you to learn more about successful communication strategies and techniques. We sincerely hope you enjoy studying and working through *Complete Communication*.

James Bury, Anthony Sellick, and Kaori Horiuchi

CONTENTS

CONTENT CHART

Focus on Function	Communication Outcomes
Using *let* to get information and make requests	Be able to provide personal information
Using *like* to describe things	Be able to provide information about hobbies and pastimes
Using *next to* to indicate position	Be able to provide information about homes and hometowns
Using *I see* and *I know* to signal understanding	Be able to provide information about families
Using *little* and *a little*	Be able to provide information and express opinions about places and sights
Different uses of *take*	Be able to provide information and express opinions about transport and directions
Question tags	Be able to provide information and express opinions about food
Using *kind of* to describe things	Be able to provide information and express opinions about restaurants and meals
Using *sound like* to react and give opinions	Be able to provide information and express opinions about movies and TV programs
Using *whose* to indicate possession	Be able to provide information and express opinions about playing and enjoying music
Quantifiers	Be able to provide information and express opinions about shops and shopping
Using *used to* to describe past activities	Be able to provide information and express opinions about sports and exercise
Using *could* to indicate possibility and ability	Be able to provide information and express opinions about travel and vacations
Using *that's why* to indicate reason and cause	Be able to provide information and express opinions about work and jobs
Using *why don't* to make suggestions and give advice	Be able to provide information and express opinions about future plans

EnglishCentralのご案内

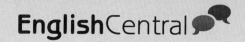

本テキスト各ユニットの「II. Warm-up for Listening & Speaking : Listening Practice 1」、「III. Conversation : Part 2」、「IV. Pronunciation Check : Exercises」で学習する音声は、オンライン学習システム「EnglishCentral」で学習することができます。

EnglishCentralでは動画の視聴や単語のディクテーションのほか、動画のセリフを音読し録音すると、コンピュータが発音を判定します。PCのwebだけでなく、スマートフォン、タブレットではアプリでも学習できます。リスニング、スピーキング、語彙力向上のため、ぜひ活用してください。

EnglishCentralの利用にはアカウントとアクセスコードの登録が必要です。登録方法については下記ページにアクセスしてください。

（画像はすべてサンプルで、実際の教材とは異なります）

https://www.seibido.co.jp/englishcentral/pdf/ectextregister.pdf

見る

本文内でわからなかった単語は1クリックでその場で意味を確認

スロー再生

日英字幕（ON/OFF可）

学ぶ

音声を聴いて空欄の単語をタイピング。ゲーム感覚で楽しく単語を覚える

動画のセリフを音読し録音、コンピュータが発音を判定。

話す

日本人向けに専門開発された音声認識によってスピーキング力を％で判定

ネイティブと自分が録音した発音を聞き比べ練習に生かすことができます

苦手な発音記号を的確に判断し、単語を緑、黄、赤の3色で表示

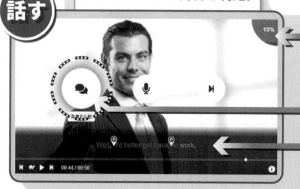

UNIT 1

Nice to meet you.
– Talking about Ourselves

I Vocabulary

● **Part 1:** Match the Japanese words (a~j) to the English words and phrases (1~10).
1～10 の語の意味として適切なものを a～j から選びましょう。

a. 話す	b. 姓	c. 言語	d. 故郷	e. 会う
f. 朝	g. 国	h. 情報	i. 字を綴る	j. お気に入りの

1. ____ hometown   2. ____ country   3. ____ meet
4. ____ morning   5. ____ speak   6. ____ spell
7. ____ family name   8. ____ favorite   9. ____ language
10. ____ information

● **Part 2:** Complete the dialogs with words and phrases from Part 1.
Part 1 の単語リストから適切な語を選んで文を完成させましょう。

1. **A:** Where are you from?
   B: I'm from the UK. My _____ is London.

2. **A:** Which _____ are you from?
   B: I'm from Japan.

3. **A:** How do you _____ your name?
   B: It's J-O-N-E-S.

4. **A:** Hello. I'm Misaki.
   B: Hello. I'm sorry, is Misaki your given name or your _____ ?

5. **A:** What's your _____ type of music?
   B: I like rap best. It's so cool!

● **Listening Practice 1:** Listen to the conversation and check (✔) the boxes next to the sentences you hear.

会話を聞いて、どちらの表現が使われているか選んでチェックを入れましょう。

Speaker A	Speaker B
☐ Hi! How are you?	
☐ Hi! Nice to meet you.	
	☐ Nice to meet you, too.
	☐ I'm fine, thank you.
☐ I'm Mariam. What's your name?	
☐ My name's Brini. What's your name?	
	☐ I'm John.
	☐ My name is John.
☐ Which country do you come from?	
☐ Where do you come from?	
	☐ I come from the US.
	☐ I'm from the UK.
Where do you live?	
	☐ I live in London.
	☐ I live in Los Angeles.
How old are you?	
	☐ I'm 21.
	☐ I'm 21 years old.

● **Speaking Practice:** Practice the conversation with your partner.

パートナーと会話を練習しましょう。

CD 3, 4

● **Listening Practice 2:** Listen to two people making short introductions. Write the speakers' names and check (✔) the correct box for each item.

2人が自己紹介をしているのを聞きましょう。話し手の名前を記入し、それぞれの情報について Yes か No を選びましょう。

1. Name: _____	Yes	No
is from Tokyo	✔	☐
speaks Spanish	☐	☐
is 29	☐	☐
likes soccer	☐	☐

2. Name: _____	Yes	No
is from New York	☐	✔
speaks Spanish	☐	☐
is 19	☐	☐
likes singing	☐	☐

III ‖ Conversation

 5

● **Part 1-1 (Get the gist):** Listen to the conversation and choose the correct answers (a~d).

会話を聞いて、最も適切なものを a ～ d の中から選びましょう。

    1. Who are Mary and Seiya most likely?
- **a.** Friends
- **b.** Co-workers
- **c.** Teacher and student
- **d.** Receptionist and student

    2. What are they mainly talking about?
- **a.** Seiya's personal information
- **b.** Mary's personal information
- **c.** Little Britain School of English
- **d.** Osaka

● **Part 1-2 (Get the details):** Listen to the conversation again and choose the correct answers (a~d).

もう一度会話を聞いて、最も適切なものを a ～ d の中から選びましょう。

    3. What does Seiya want to do?
- **a.** Start an English course
- **b.** Get some information about Mary
- **c.** Go to Osaka
- **d.** Go to Manchester

    4. What does Mary ask Seiya to do?
- **a.** Start an English course
- **b.** Spell his given name
- **c.** Spell his family name
- **d.** Spell his hometown

● **Part 2:** Listen to the conversation again and write the missing words or phrases in the spaces.

会話をもう一度聞いて、空欄に適語を書き入れましょう。

Mary: Good morning. My name is Mary. (1) _____ to Little Britain School of English.

Seiya: Good morning. My name is Seiya. I want to start an English course.

Mary: Ok, great! (2) _____ _____ _____ _____, Seiya. Let me ask you for some more information about yourself.

Seiya: Sure, no (3) _____.

Mary: Your given name is Seiya. What's your (4) _____ _____?

Seiya: It's Fukushima.

Mary: How do you (5) _____ that?

Seiya: F-U-K-U-S-H-I-M-A.

Mary: Where are you from?

Seiya: I'm from Osaka in Japan, but I (6) _____ in Manchester now.

● **Speaking Practice:** Practice the conversation with your partner.

パートナーと一緒に会話を練習しましょう。

IV ▌Pronunciation Check

強弱に注意しよう！

英語には強く発音するところと、弱く発音するところがあって、リズミカルに聞こえます。会話の中で大事なポイントは強く、そうでない部分は弱く発音されています。このリズムに慣れると、内容を理解しやすくなってきます。

例）I want to start an English course. ［下線部の語が強く発音されています］

強弱を意識して、発音の練習をしてみましょう。

Exercises

 6

● **Listen to the recording and underline the stressed words in the sentences below. Then, practice saying the sentences, paying attention to stress.**

以下の文で強調する単語に下線を引きましょう。次に、音声を聞いて解答を確認します。強弱に注意しながら、文章を読む練習をしましょう。

  1. He lives in Seattle with his family.

  2. I want to speak Spanish well.

  3. Dublin is my hometown. It's a beautiful old city.

V ▌Focus on Function

Let me . . . 「〜させてください」

相手に質問するときには、Do you . . . ? What is your . . . ? など疑問文を使うことが多いと思います。しかし、疑問文ではない形 Let me ask you . . . という表現も、何かを尋ねるときに使える言い回しです。Dialog のなかで Mary が Seiya に「あなたについてもっと質問させてください」と言っていましたね。少しフォーマルな言い方なので、初対面の人と話す場合に適しています。ask を別の動詞にして、「私に〜させてください」という使い方もできます。

Exercises

● **Translate the Japanese sentences below into English using *let*.**

日本文に合うように、let を使って英文を完成させましょう。

  1. 質問させてください。

   _____ me _____ you a _____.

  2. 一緒に行かせてください。

   _____ me _____ _____ you.

  3. あなたの到着時間を教えてください。

   Please _____ me _____ the time of _____

   _____.

VI | Find out

● **Find out about your classmates. Ask three people the following questions.**

クラスメートに質問してみましょう。3人に聞いて、答えを書いてください。

	Partner 1	Partner 2	Partner 3
1. What's your name?			
2. Where are you from?			
3. Where do you live?			
4. How old are you?			
5. What languages do you speak?			
6. What's your favorite _____?			
7. Your question: _____?			

Useful Language

Questions
- What is . . . ?
- Where are you from?
- Where do you live?

Answers
- I am . . . / It is . . .
- I am from . . .
- I live in . . .

Details
- Countries: the UK / the US / Japan / Canada / the Philippines / China / Kenya
- Cities: London / Los Angeles / Tokyo / Toronto / Manila / Beijing / Nairobi

Notes

場所を尋ねるときには where を使います。出身地を聞く場合は、Where are you from? と最後に前置詞の from をつけますが、住んでいる場所を聞くときには、Where do you live? と最後に前置詞はつけません。答えるときには、I live in . . .と前置詞をつけます。

UNIT 2

What do you like to do?
– Talking about Hobbies and Pastimes

I Vocabulary

● **Part 1:** Match the Japanese words (a~j) to the English words and phrases (1~10).
1 ～ 10 の語の意味として適切なものを a ～ j から選びましょう。

a. 自由時間	b. 練習する	c. チームメイト	d. 週末	e. 友好的な
f. クラブ、部活	g. 趣味	h. 毎日	i. 集める	j. 練習

1. ____ hobby   2. ____ weekend   3. ____ club
4. ____ practice（動）   5. ____ practice（名）   6. ____ clubmate
7. ____ collect   8. ____ free time   9. ____ every day
10. ____ friendly

● **Part 2:** Complete the dialogs with words and phrases from Part 1.
Part 1 の単語リストから適切な語を選んで文を完成させましょう。

1. **A:** What's your hobby or pastime?
   B: I _____ stamps from different places in Japan.

2. **A:** What do you like to do on the _____?
   B: I like to relax at home and watch TV.

3. **A:** Do you like your club activities?
   B: Yes! My _____ are all really friendly.

4. **A:** What do you do in your _____?
   B: I like to listen to music.

5. **A:** How often do you do your hobby?
   B: I do it _____! I love it!

Note: stamps：駅や観光地などに置いてある記念のスタンプ、寺社の朱印などのこと。

II ┃ Warm-up for Listening & Speaking

 EC CD 7

● **Listening Practice 1:** Listen to the conversation and check (✔) the boxes next to the sentences you hear.

会話を聞いて、どちらの表現が使われているか選んでチェックを入れましょう。

Speaker A	Speaker B
☐ Hi, Shane. Where are you going? ☐ Hello, Shane. What are you doing?	
	I'm going to my club practice. ☐ I'm going to meet my clubmates. ☐
☐ What club are you in? ☐ Which club do you belong to?	
	I'm in the baseball club. ☐ I'm in the basketball club. ☐
☐ When did you join that club? ☐ When does your practice start?	
	In 30 minutes. ☐ Two years ago. ☐
How often do you practice?	
	Every day. ☐ Three times a week. ☐
Is it fun?	
	Yes, sure. ☐ Yes, I love it! ☐

● **Speaking Practice:** Practice the conversation with your partner.

パートナーと会話を練習しましょう。

CD 8, 9

● **Listening Practice 2:** Listen to two people talking about their hobbies. Write the hobbies and check (✔) the correct box for each item.

2人が趣味について話しているのを聞きましょう。どのような趣味かを記入し、それぞれの情報について Yes か No を選びましょう。

1. Hobby: _____

	Yes	No
started in high school	✔	☐
practices every day	☐	☐
finds it difficult	☐	☐
likes it	☐	☐

2. Hobby: _____

	Yes	No
started in high school	☐	✔
does it every day	☐	☐
finds it difficult	☐	☐
likes it	☐	☐

III Conversation

 10

● **Part 1-1 (Get the gist):** Listen to the conversation and choose the correct answers (a~d).

会話を聞いて、最も適切なものを a～d の中から選びましょう。

1. Who are Sarah and Masayuki most likely?

    a. Friends

    b. Clubmates

    c. Teacher and student

    d. Brother and sister

2. Where are they most likely talking?

    a. In class

    b. At a kendo club

    c. At a restaurant

    d. Outside a classroom

● **Part 1-2 (Get the details):** Listen to the conversation again and choose the correct answers (a~d).

もう一度会話を聞いて、最も適切なものを a～d の中から選びましょう。

3. What does Sarah say about Masayuki's bag?

    a. It's big

    b. It's heavy

    c. It's for karate

    d. It's for kendo

4. When does Masayuki sometimes have a kendo tournament?

    a. Every day

    b. On Mondays

    c. On Thursdays

    d. On the weekend

Part 2: Listen to the conversation again and write the missing words or phrases in the spaces.

会話をもう一度聞いて、空欄に適語を書き入れましょう。

Sarah: Hi, Masayuki. That's a big bag. What's in it?

Masayuki: Hi, Sarah. It's my kendo training kit. It's really **(1)** _____.

Sarah: Kendo? **(2)** _____ _____?

Masayuki: It's a kind of Japanese martial art.

Sarah: Oh, like karate or judo?

Masayuki: A bit, but we **(3)** _____ a bamboo sword called a *shinai*. We wear protection, too.

Sarah: How **(4)** _____ _____ _____ practice?

Masayuki: Every day except Monday and Thursday. **(5)** _____ we have a tournament on the weekend.

Sarah: Wow! That sounds like very hard **(6)** _____. You must hate it!

Masayuki: No! It is hard and I don't get much free time, but my clubmates are really friendly, so I love it! I always want to do kendo!

Speaking Practice: Practice the conversation with your partner.

パートナーと一緒に会話を練習しましょう。

IV ┃Pronunciation Check

be 動詞の短縮形

会話の中では、apostrophe（アポストロフィ）を使って表現される短縮形がよく使われます。
be 動詞が主語と結びついて短くなった発音に気をつけましょう。

例）That is a big bag. → That's a big bag.
　　It is my textbook. → It's my textbook.
　　What is that? → What's that?［疑問詞と結びつくこともあります］
　　＊ This is は This's と s が重なるため、基本的に短縮形を使いません。

Exercises

 11

● **Look at the sentences below and circle the ones you hear. Then, practice saying
the sentences, paying attention to contractions.**

以下の英文を見て、聞こえたほうを丸で囲みましょう。答えを確認し、短縮形に注意しながら文章を読
んで練習しましょう。

　1. She is a good doctor. / She's a good doctor.

　2. I am looking for my smartphone. / I'm looking for my smartphone.

　3. I think you are really great. / I think you're really great.

V ┃Focus on Function

like「～のような」

like は動詞の「好む」の他に、前置詞の「～のような、～のように」という意味があります。
like ＋名詞の形で、似ているものを示して例えるときに使います。動詞との違いに注意して、
使い方を覚えましょう。

例）This fruit is sour like a lemon.（この果物はレモンのように酸っぱい）
　　It is shaped like a star.（それは星のような形をしている）

Exercises

● **Translate the Japanese sentences below into English using *like*.**

日本文に合うように、like を使って英文を完成させましょう。

　1. ポールとウェズリーは兄弟のようだ。

　　Paul and Wesley are ＿＿＿＿＿＿＿ ＿＿＿＿＿＿＿.

　2. 彼女は裕福で、夢のような暮らしをしている。

　　She is rich, and her life is ＿＿＿＿＿＿＿ ＿＿＿＿＿＿＿ ＿＿＿＿＿＿＿.

　3. このような車が欲しいです。

　　I'd like a car ＿＿＿＿＿＿＿ ＿＿＿＿＿＿＿.

VI │ Find out

● **Find out about your classmates. Ask three people the following questions.**

クラスメートに質問してみましょう。3人に聞いて、答えを書いてください。

	Partner 1	Partner 2	Partner 3
1. What's your hobby?			
2. Where do you do it?			
3. Who do you do it with?			
4. How often do you do it?			
5. When did you start doing it?			
6. Is it easy to do?			
7. Your question: _____?			

Useful Language

Questions
- What's your . . . ?
- When did you start . . . ?
- Is it easy to . . . ?

Answers
- My . . . is (or are) . . . / I like . . . / I enjoy . . .
- I started when I was . . .
- Yes, it is. / No, it isn't.

Details
- Activities: reading / watching movies / camping / playing the piano / gardening / collecting trading cards / traveling

Notes
趣味について聞かれたら、My hobbies are . . . と答えても良いですし、I like . . . や I enjoy . . . と答えることもできます。enjoy を使うときには、後ろに名詞または動詞を -ing の形にしたものが続きます。to 不定詞は使えないので注意しましょう。

UNIT 3

Where are you from?
– Talking about Hometowns

I Vocabulary

● **Part 1:** Match the Japanese words (a~j) to the English words and phrases (1~10).
1～10 の語の意味として適切なものを a～j から選びましょう。

a. 西	b. 育つ	c. 引っ越す	d. 南	e. 近い
f. 遠い	g. 北	h. 県	i. 東	j. 旅行

1. ____ north
2. ____ south
3. ____ east
4. ____ west
5. ____ near
6. ____ far
7. ____ grow up
8. ____ prefecture
9. ____ move
10. ____ trip

● **Part 2:** Complete the dialogs with words and phrases from Part 1.
Part 1 の単語リストから適切な語を選んで文を完成させましょう。

1. **A:** Did you _____ in New York?
   B: No, I didn't. I'm from California.

2. **A:** Have you always lived in Tokyo?
   B: Yes, I have, but I will _____ to Iwate next year.

3. **A:** I'm going on a(n) _____ to Osaka next week.
   B: Really? That's my hometown.

4. **A:** Okay, let's study Japanese history. What was the old name of Niigata _____?
   B: I know! It was *Echigo no kuni*.

5. **A:** I'm from Sapporo in the north of Japan. How about you?
   B: I'm from Naha in the _____ of Japan.

● **Listening Practice 1:** Listen to the conversation and check (✔) the boxes next to the sentences you hear.

会話を聞いて、どちらの表現が使われているか選んでチェックを入れましょう。

Speaker A	Speaker B
☐ Where's your hometown? ☐ Where are you from?	
	I'm not sure. ☐ That's difficult to say. ☐
☐ Why's that? ☐ Really? How come?	
	I've moved lots of times. ☐ I think I've moved about 10 times. ☐
☐ Wow! I've never moved. ☐ Hmm. Which place did you like best?	
	I live in Tokyo now. It's so exciting. ☐ I think I liked Naha best. ☐
Then that's your hometown!	That sounds good. ☐ I think so, too. ☐
Why don't you visit my hometown sometime?	
	Thanks. I'd love to take a trip there.

● **Speaking Practice:** Practice the conversation with your partner.

パートナーと会話を練習しましょう。

🎧 13, 14

● **Listening Practice 2:** Listen to two people talk about their hometowns. Write the speakers' names and check (✔) the correct box for each item.

2人の故郷の話を聞きましょう。話し手の名前を書き、それぞれの情報について Yes か No を選びましょう。

1. Name: _____

	Yes	No
lives in Osaka	✔	☐
is from Niseko	☐	☐
likes Osaka	☐	☐
likes Disneyland	☐	☐

2. Name: _____

	Yes	No
lives in London	☐	✔
is from Manchester	☐	☐
likes Fukuoka	☐	☐
likes Japan	☐	☐

III ‖Conversation

 15

● **Part 1-1 (Get the gist):** Listen to the conversation and choose the correct answers (a~d).

会話を聞いて、最も適切なものを a ～ d の中から選びましょう。

  1. What are Anthony and Miwa mainly talking about?
       a. Anthony's hometown
       b. Miwa's hometown
       c. Chiba Prefecture
       d. Nara Prefecture

  2. What will Anthony probably do?
       a. Travel to Tsu City
       b. Go to London
       c. Move to Ichikawa City
       d. Visit Chiba Prefecture

● **Part 1-2 (Get the details):** Listen to the conversation again and choose the correct answers (a~d).

もう一度会話を聞いて、最も適切なものを a ～ d の中から選びましょう。

  3. Where did Anthony think Miwa was from?
       a. Ichikawa City
       b. London
       c. Tsu City
       d. Nara Prefecture

  4. Where is Miwa from?
       a. Nara Prefecture
       b. Chiba Prefecture
       c. Ichikawa City
       d. Tsu City

15

● **Part 2:** Listen to the conversation again and write the missing words or phrases in the spaces.

会話をもう一度聞いて、空欄に適語を書き入れましょう。

Anthony: Where do you live, Miwa?

Miwa: I (1) _____ _____ Ichikawa City.

Anthony: Me, too! So, Ichikawa City is your (2) _____.

Miwa: Oh, no. I moved to Chiba Prefecture for college.

Anthony: Yeah, so (3) _____ _____. I'm from London. Where's your hometown?

Miwa: I'm from Tsu City in Mie Prefecture. So, you're from England, Anthony?

Anthony: Yes, I'm English. Miwa, I'm really sorry, but I don't know where Tsu City is. Is it near Chiba Prefecture?

Miwa: No, it's quite far. It's east of Nara Prefecture. It's next to the (4) _____. You can see the sea from my home.

Anthony: That (5) _____ nice. I'd like to see where you grew up someday.

Miwa: Really? How about this (6) _____?

● **Speaking Practice:** Practice the conversation with your partner.

パートナーと一緒に会話を練習しましょう。

IV Pronunciation Check

see, sea, she の発音

英語では綴りが違うけれども同じ発音や、似ているけれども違う発音の単語があります。
動詞の see「見る」と名詞の sea「海」は、両方とも同じ発音【siː】です。アルファベットの
C もこれと同じです。人称代名詞の she「彼女は」は、違う発音【ʃiː】となります。
これらの単語を使った有名な早口言葉があります。
例）She sells sea shells by the seashore.（彼女は海岸で貝殻を売っている）
日本人には違いが難しい発音ですが、意識して練習してみましょう。

Exercises

 16

● Look at the sentences below and circle the words that you hear. Then, practice
saying the sentences, paying attention to the sounds /ʃiː/ and /siː/.

以下の英文を見て、聞こえたほうを丸で囲みましょう。音声を聞いて正しい発音をチェックし、【ʃiː】
と【siː】に気をつけながらもう一度練習しましょう。

    1. (**She / see**) can (**she / see**) the (**she / sea**) from her home.

    2. (**She / see**) put her (**sheets / seats**) on the (**sheet / seat**).

    3. (**She / see**) never thought (**she / see**) would (**she / see**) such a beautiful scene.

V Focus on Function

next to「～の隣」

並んでいる物や人などの位置を説明するときに、next to を使います。比較的近い場所で、隣接
している場合に使う表現です。道を尋ねられて、案内するときにも便利なフレーズです。
例）My house is next to the park.（私の家は公園に隣接しています）
    She was standing next to Antonio.（彼女はアントニオの隣に立っていました）

Exercises

● Translate the Japanese sentences below into English using *next to.*

日本文に合うように、next to を使って英文を完成させましょう。

    1. 駅の隣に観光案内所があります。
    There is a visitor center ＿＿＿＿＿＿＿ ＿＿＿＿＿＿＿ ＿＿＿＿＿＿＿
    ＿＿＿＿＿＿＿.

    2. エマはケンジの隣に座っています。
    Emma is ＿＿＿＿＿＿＿ ＿＿＿＿＿＿＿ ＿＿＿＿＿＿＿ Kenji.

    3. あの大きな木の隣にある建物が、私たちの学校です。
    The ＿＿＿＿＿＿＿ ＿＿＿＿＿＿＿ ＿＿＿＿＿＿＿ the big tree is our
    school.

VI Find out

● **Find out about your classmates. Ask three people the following questions.**
クラスメートに質問してみましょう。3人に聞いて、答えを書いてください。

	Partner 1	Partner 2	Partner 3
1. Where is your hometown?			
2. Where do you live now?			
3. How long have you lived there?			
4. Who do you live with?			
5. How many times have you moved?			
6. Where do you want to live?			
7. Your question: _____?			

Useful Language

Questions
- Where is . . . ?
- Where do you . . . ?
- Who do you live with?

Answers
- It is . . .
- I live in . . .
- I live with . . .

Details
- People: parents / mother / father / brother / sister / grandmother / grandfather / roommate
- Locations: north / south / east / west / near / far / prefecture / town / city
- Actions: grow up / move / take a trip / visit

Notes
誰と住んでいるかを尋ねるときは、Who do you live with? と、「一緒に」という意味の前置詞 with を付けます。答えるときは I live with my sister. のように、with の後に人物を示します。過去のことを尋ねるときは Who did you live with? と聞いて、答えるときは I lived with . . . と答えましょう。

UNIT 4

Who's that?
– Talking about Family

I Vocabulary

● **Part 1:** Match the Japanese words (a~j) to the English words (1~10).

1～10 の語の意味として適切なものを a ～ j から選びましょう。

a. 親	b. 母	c. 兄・弟	d. 妻	e. 夫
f. 姉・妹	g. 年長の	h. 子どもたち	i. 年下の	j. 父

1. ____ father

2. ____ mother

3. ____ parent(s)

4. ____ children

5. ____ brother

6. ____ sister

7. ____ husband

8. ____ wife

9. ____ younger

10. ____ older

● **Part 2:** Complete the dialogs with words from Part 1.

Part 1 の単語リストから適切な語を選んで文を完成させましょう。

1. **A:** How did your _____ meet?
   B: They went to school together.

2. **A:** Who's that?
   B: That's my uncle. He's my father's _____.

3. **A:** Who's that?
   B: She's my aunt. She's my father's _____.

4. **A:** Are you _____ or younger than your wife?
   B: I'm one year younger than her. I'm 35 and she's 36.

5. **A:** How many _____ do you want to have?
   B: We want to have two, a girl and a boy.

II Warm-up for Listening & Speaking

 17

● **Listening Practice 1:** Listen to the conversation and check (✔) the boxes next to the sentences you hear.

会話を聞いて、どちらの表現が使われているか選んでチェックを入れましょう。

Speaker A	Speaker B

☐ Who's that?
☐ What's that?

☐ This is a picture of my sister.
☐ That's my sister.

☐ She's really cute.
☐ She's very good looking.

Thanks.

☐ Is she older or younger than you?
☐ Are you older or younger than her?

I'm five years younger than her.

Do you have any other brothers or sisters?

☐ Yes, I do. I have an older brother, too. How about you?
☐ No, I don't. How about you?

☐ Yes, I do. I have three brothers and two sisters.
☐ Yes, I do. I have three sisters and two brothers.

Wow! You have a big family, don't you?

● **Speaking Practice:** Practice the conversation with your partner.

パートナーと会話を練習しましょう。

18, 19

● **Listening Practice 2:** Listen to two people talking about their families. Write the speakers' names and check (✔) the correct box for each item.

家族について２人が話しているのを聞きましょう。話し手の名前を書き、それぞれの情報について Yes か No を選びましょう。

1. Name: _____

	Yes	No
is from Malaysia	✔	☐
has a big family	☐	☐
has two sisters	☐	☐
has a pet	☐	☐

2. Name: _____

	Yes	No
is from America	☐	☐
has a big family	☐	☐
has two brothers	☐	☐
has a pet	☐	☐

III Conversation

 20

● **Part 1-1 (Get the gist):** Listen to the conversation and choose the correct answers (a~d).

会話を聞いて、最も適切なものを a～d の中から選びましょう。

1. How does Martin probably feel about Anna's family?

    a. Happy

    b. Surprised

    c. Angry

    d. Sad

2. What do we know about Martin's and Anna's families?

    a. They are both large.

    b. They are both small.

    c. Martin's family is larger.

    d. Anna's family is larger.

● **Part 1-2 (Get the details):** Listen to the conversation again and choose the correct answers (a~d).

もう一度会話を聞いて、最も適切なものを a～d の中から選びましょう。

3. How many brothers and sisters does Anna have?

    a. 3

    b. 4

    c. 7

    d. 8

4. What do we know about Anna?

    a. She is Martin's sister.

    b. She is a university student.

    c. She has eight children.

    d. She is married.

● **Part 2:** Listen to the conversation again and write the missing words or phrases in the spaces.

会話をもう一度聞いて、空欄に適語を書き入れましょう。

Martin: Do you have a big family, Anna?

Anna: Yes, I do. My parents had (1) _____ children. I have three brothers and four sisters.

Martin: Wow, that's a lot. (2) _____ _____ _____. That's only seven children.

Anna: Don't (3) _____ about me, Martin! How about you? Do you have any brothers or sisters?

Martin: Yes, I do. I have a younger brother. He's studying at university now.

Anna: I always wanted to have a younger brother. I only have younger sisters and (4) _____ brothers.

Martin: I can't imagine what it's like to live in such a big family.

Anna: Well, you're never (5) _____, which is nice. On the (6) _____ _____, you are never alone.

Martin: Ha ha. I see. How about your husband? Does he have a big family, too?

Anna: He does now!

● **Speaking Practice:** Practice the conversation with your partner.

パートナーと一緒に会話を練習しましょう。

22

IV │Pronunciation Check

つながる音　t ＋母音

英語のリスニングで正確に聞き取ったり、ネイティブスピーカーのように発音したりするためには、単語をつなげて発音する音声変化に注意する必要があります。いくつかのパターンがありますが、今回は t ＋母音の形を覚えておきましょう。アルファベットの t で終わる単語の次に母音で始まる単語が続くとき、つなげて発音します。

例）Wait a moment.［下線部の箇所がつなげて発音されます］

Exercises

 21

● Listen to the recording and connect the linked words using ‿ in the sentences below. Then, practice saying the sentences, paying attention to linking.

音声を聞いて、つながる音に印 (‿) を付けましょう。その後、つながる音に注意して発音を練習してみましょう。

1. I got up at six this morning.

2. What do you think about it?

3. She put on her raincoat because it started raining.

V │Focus on Function

I see. 相手に理解を示す

相手の話していることに対して、上手に応答できるとスムーズに会話が進みます。"I see." は、「なるほど」、「わかりました」という意味で、会話で頻繁に使われるフレーズです。後ろに what you mean をつけて、"I see what you mean." 「おっしゃる通りです」という言い方は、ビジネスの場でよく使用されます。他にも "I know." というフレーズがありますが、こちらは「そうですね」、「わかります」という意味です。すでに知っていることについて、理解を示すためのフレーズです。

Exercises

● Look at the sentences below and write a reply.

英文に対して、理解を示す応答をしてみましょう。

1. **A:** I lost my smartphone, so I couldn't contact you.
   B: _____.

2. **A:** Samuel is a nice teacher. He always speaks kindly to his students.
   B: _____.

3. **A:** Our company should take action to improve sales.
   B: _____.

VI ‖ Find out

● **Find out about your classmates. Ask three people the following questions.**

クラスメートに質問してみましょう。3人に聞いて、答えを書いてください。

	Partner 1	Partner 2	Partner 3
1. How many people are there in your family?			
2. Do you have any brothers or sisters?			
3. How old is your father?			
4. What does your mother do?			
5. Where do your parents live?			
6. Do you have any pets?			
7. Your question: _____?			

UNIT 5

Where's that?
– Talking about Places and Sights

I ┃ Vocabulary

● **Part 1: Match the Japanese words (a~j) to the English words (1~10).**

1 ～ 10 の語の意味として適切なものを a ～ j から選びましょう。

a. 印象的な	b. 博物館	c. 推薦する	d. 噴水・泉	e. 人気のある
f. 競技場	g. 彫像	h. 興味深い	i. 有名な	j. 券

1. ____ museum   2. ____ statue   3. ____ fountain
4. ____ stadium   5. ____ recommend   6. ____ ticket
7. ____ impressive   8. ____ interesting   9. ____ famous
10. ____ popular

● **Part 2: Complete the dialogs with words from Part 1.**

Part 1 の単語リストから適切な語を選んで文を完成させましょう。

1. **A:** I want to see the _____ of Hachiko in Shibuya.
    B: Yes, it's very famous.

2. **A:** Where are all these people going to?
    B: To the _____. There's a big soccer game there today.

3. **A:** I want to visit Disneyland. How much is a(n) _____?
    B: A 1-day passport is ¥8,200 for adults.

4. **A:** I'm going to Tokyo soon. Where do you _____ I go?
    B: I think you should go to the Shitamachi Museum in Ueno.

5. **A:** Why is the museum so _____ with tourists?
    B: Because it's really big, interesting, and free.

● **Listening Practice 1:** Listen to the conversation and check (✔) the boxes next to the sentences you hear.

会話を聞いて、どちらの表現が使われているか選んでチェックを入れましょう。

Speaker A	Speaker B
☐ Where do you recommend I visit here?	
☐ Where's a good place to visit here?	
	I recommend the history museum. ☐
	You should go to the history museum. ☐
☐ That sounds interesting. Where is it?	
☐ I'd like to go there. Where is it?	
	It's in the city center, near the fountain. ☐
	Next to the train station. ☐
☐ Where else is good?	
☐ Is there anywhere else I should go?	
	The stadium is very popular. ☐
	The statue is really impressive. ☐
Will I need a ticket to go there?	
	Yes, but they're easy to buy. ☐
	No, it's outside and free. ☐
Would you like to come?	
	Yes, sure. ☐
	Sorry, I'm busy. ☐

● **Speaking Practice:** Practice the conversation with your partner.

パートナーと会話を練習しましょう。

 23, 24

● **Listening Practice 2:** Listen to two people talking about places they visited. Write the places and check (✔) the correct box for each item.

訪れたことのある場所について2人が話しているのを聞きましょう。場所を記入し、それぞれの情報について Yes か No を選びましょう。

1. Place: _____

	Yes	No
is big	☐	✔
is interesting	☐	☐
would recommend	☐	☐
need a ticket	☐	☐

2. Place: _____

	Yes	No
is big	☐	☐
is interesting	☐	☐
would recommend	☐	☐
need a ticket	☐	☐

III Conversation

 25

● **Part 1-1 (Get the gist):** Listen to the conversation and choose the correct answers (a~d).

会話を聞いて、最も適切なものを a ～ d の中から選びましょう。

1. Why was Safi surprised?

    a. Kyoto is Manami's hometown.

    b. Manami likes Kyoto.

    c. Kinkakuji is expensive to visit.

    d. He has never been to Kyoto before.

2. What will Safi probably do?

    a. Look at places to go in Kyoto

    b. Go to Manami's home

    c. Visit Gion

    d. Visit Kinkakuji

● **Part 1-2 (Get the details):** Listen to the conversation again and choose the correct answers (a~d).

もう一度会話を聞いて、最も適切なものを a ～ d の中から選びましょう。

3. What does Safi say he didn't know?

    a. Gion is popular.

    b. Kiyomizudera is popular.

    c. The name of the golden temple

    d. It is a little expensive to visit Kinkakuji.

4. Where does Manami recommend Safi visit?

    a. Gion

    b. Kiyomizudera

    c. Ginkakuji

    d. Kinkakuji

● **Part 2:** Listen to the conversation again and write the missing words or phrases in the spaces.

会話をもう一度聞いて、空欄に適語を書き入れましょう。

Manami: Hi, Safi. How's it (1)_____?

Safi: I'm good, thanks, Manami. I'm looking at (2) _____ to visit in Kyoto.

Manami: Kyoto? That's my hometown!

Safi: No way! Great! Where (3) _____ _____ _____ I visit?

Manami: Well, there are lots of (4) _____ places there. Gion, Kiyomizudera, and Ginkakuji are very popular, but my favorite place is Kinkakuji.

Safi: Why? What's there?

Manami: There's a golden temple. You must have seen (5) _____ of it.

Safi: Yes, I think I have, but I didn't know the name.

Manami: It's a little expensive to get in, but (6) _____ _____ _____ _____ go there.

Safi: OK, I will! I can't wait!

● **Speaking Practice:** Practice the conversation with your partner.

パートナーと一緒に会話を練習しましょう。

IV ‖Pronunciation Check

強調する語

相手に伝えたい情報は、ほかの箇所よりも強く、あるいは長めに発音することがあります。同じ文章でも、会話の内容に合わせて話し手が重要だと思う語句が強調されます。

例）太字の箇所を強く発音します。

There are **lots** of famous places there.　　[たくさんあることが重要なとき]
There are lots of **famous** places there.　　[有名であることが重要なとき]
There are lots of famous **places** there.　　[場所が重要なとき]

Exercises

● **Listen to the recording and circle the stressed words. Then, practice saying the sentences, paying attention to stress.**

音声を聞いて、重要な情報を選びましょう。強調する語に注意して、発音を練習してみましょう。

1. Tina's car is bigger than mine.　　**a.** car　　**b.** bigger　　**c.** mine

2. He bought five apples yesterday.　　**a.** bought　　**b.** five　　**c.** apples

3. Michael won a prize in a contest.　　**a.** Michael　　**b.** won　　**c.** prize

V ‖Focus on Function

a little 「少し」

程度や量が「ほんの少し」であるとき、"a little" を使います。数えられない名詞（不可算名詞）を修飾します。数えられる名詞（可算名詞）には使えません。"a" を省いて "little" だけだと「ほとんどない」という意味になります。

例）The coat was a little expensive.（そのコートは少し高かった）
　　He had little money.（彼はお金をほとんど持っていなかった）

Exercises

● **Translate the Japanese sentences below into English using *a little* or *little*.**

日本文に合うように、a little または little を空欄に入れましょう。

1. ボールに小麦粉を入れて、水を少し加えます。
   Put flour into a bowl and add ＿＿＿＿＿＿＿＿ water.

2. 彼らが成功する望みはほとんどない。
   They have ＿＿＿＿＿＿＿＿ hope of success.

3. この問題は私には少し難しい。
   This exercise is ＿＿＿＿＿＿＿＿ difficult for me.

VI Find out

● **Find out about your classmates. Ask three people the following questions.**

クラスメートに質問してみましょう。3人に聞いて、答えを書いてください。

	Partner 1	Partner 2	Partner 3
1. What is the best place you have ever visited?			
2. Do you like visiting different places?			
3. Where would you recommend a tourist in your country to visit?			
4. What is the most famous place in your hometown?			
5. Which place would you like to visit in the future?			
6. Do you prefer natural places (like mountains) or man-made places (like buildings)?			
7. Your question: _____?			

Useful Language

Questions

- What is the best . . . ?
- Do you like . . . ing?
- What is the most . . . ?

Answers

- I recommend . . .
- Yes, I do. / No, I don't.
- It is . . .

Details

- Places and sights: museum / zoo / park / aquarium / station / tower / temple / shrine / palace / lake / harbor / art gallery

Notes

お勧めのものを紹介するときは、"I recommend . . ." という表現を使いましょう。"I recommend Tokyo Skytree." のように、後ろに名詞を続けます。なぜ勧めたいのか "because . . ." を使って説明できると、さらに会話がうまく繋がっていきます。

UNIT 6

How do we get there?
– Talking about Transportation and Directions

I Vocabulary

🔵 **Part 1:** Match the Japanese words (a~j) to the English words and phrases (1~10).

1～10の語の意味として適切なものを a～j から選びましょう。

a. （乗り物に）乗る	b. 後ろに	c. 新幹線	d. ～の前に	e. （角を）曲がる
f. 連絡船	g. 反対側の	h. ～の隣	i. ～の間	j. ～の近くに

1. ＿＿＿ ferry 　　　　2. ＿＿＿ next to 　　　　3. ＿＿＿ opposite

4. ＿＿＿ turn 　　　　5. ＿＿＿ take 　　　　6. ＿＿＿ bullet train

7. ＿＿＿ between 　　　8. ＿＿＿ in front of 　　9. ＿＿＿ behind

10. ＿＿＿ near

🔵 **Part 2:** Complete the dialogs with words and phrases from Part 1.

Part 1 の単語リストから適切な語を選んで文を完成させましょう。

1. **A:** Oh, no. We're going to be late!
   B: Don't worry. We can ＿＿＿＿＿＿＿ a taxi.

2. **A:** How was your trip to Europe?
   B: It was amazing. I took a(n) ＿＿＿＿＿＿＿ across Lake Geneva from France to Switzerland.

3. **A:** Is Manchester ＿＿＿＿＿＿＿ to your hometown?
   B: No, it's not. It's about 150 km away.

4. **A:** How do we get to your house?
   B: ＿＿＿＿＿＿＿ right at the traffic lights and then go straight.

5. **A:** How long does it take to travel from Tokyo to Osaka by ＿＿＿＿＿＿＿?
   B: It takes about two and a half hours.

● Listening Practice 1: Listen to the conversation and check (✔) the boxes next to the sentences you hear.

会話を聞いて、どちらの表現が使われているか選んでチェックを入れましょう。

Speaker A	Speaker B
☐ Can you tell me how to get to the station, please?	
☐ Excuse me. Do you know where the museum is?	
	Of course. Take the first right. ☐
	Sure. Go straight and then turn left. ☐
Uh huh.	
	Then take the second left. ☐
	Turn right at the bakery. ☐
Right.	
	Go past the park. ☐
	Then turn left at the post office. ☐
Okay.	
	It's next to the movie theater. ☐
	It's between the hospital and the school. ☐
☐ Is it far?	
☐ How far is it?	
	It takes about 10 minutes on foot. ☐
	It'll take less than 10 minutes. ☐

● Speaking Practice: Practice the conversation with your partner.

パートナーと会話を練習しましょう。

 28, 29

● Listening Practice 2: Listen to two people give directions to different places. Write the places and check (✔) the correct box for each item.

ある場所への行き方について2人の説明を聞きましょう。場所を記入し、それぞれの情報について Yes か No を選びましょう。

1. Place: _____

	Yes	No
go straight	✔	☐
turn right	☐	☐
turn right	☐	☐
on the left	☐	☐

2. Place: _____

	Yes	No
third left	☐	☐
second right	☐	☐
second right	☐	☐
on the right	☐	☐

III ‖Conversation

 30

● **Part 1-1 (Get the gist):** Listen to the conversation and choose the correct answers (a~d).

会話を聞いて、最も適切なものを a〜d の中から選びましょう。

1. What will Yuzuki and John most likely do?

   a. They will meet at a party this evening.

   b. They will work in a restaurant this evening.

   c. They will go to a supermarket this evening.

   d. They will meet six friends this evening.

2. What do we know about John?

   a. He usually takes a taxi to the restaurant.

   b. He has been to the restaurant before.

   c. He works part time in the restaurant.

   d. He knows where the restaurant is.

● **Part 1-2 (Get the details):** Listen to the conversation again and choose the correct answers (a~d).

もう一度会話を聞いて、最も適切なものを a〜d の中から選びましょう。

3. Which of the following directions is correct?

   a. Go straight. First right. First left. It's on the left.

   b. Go straight. First right. First left. It's on the right.

   c. Go straight. Second right. First left. It's on the left.

   d. Go straight. Second left. First right. It's on the right.

4. If the weather is bad, what should Yuzuki do?

   a. She should drive.

   b. She should walk.

   c. She should take a taxi or a bus.

   d. She should wait.

30

Part 2: Listen to the conversation again and write the missing words or phrases in the spaces.

会話をもう一度聞いて、空欄に適語を書き入れましょう。

Yuzuki: Hey John, are you going to Yuka's party tonight?

John: Oh, hi Yuzuki. Yes, I am. Do you know how to get to the restaurant?

Yuzuki: No, I don't. Can you give me some (1) _____?

John: Sure. First, you need to (2) _____ _____ _____ from Yachiyo to Ichikawa City.

Yuzuki: Okay. Which exit do I need to go to?

John: The north exit. You (3) _____ get to the restaurant from the south exit. From there, go straight and take the second left. There is a bus stop just before the corner, in front of a convenience store.

Yuzuki: Go straight and turn left at the bus stop? Got it.

John: Then turn right. The restaurant is (4) _____ _____ _____, maybe two or three hundred meters down the road. It's (5) _____ a supermarket.

Yuzuki: That doesn't sound too hard. I'm sure I can find it.

John: If it rains, you should take a (6) _____ or a bus from the station. It only takes a few minutes.

Yuzuki: Thanks. See you there at six.

Speaking Practice: Practice the conversation with your partner.

パートナーと一緒に会話を練習しましょう。

IV ‖Pronunciation Check

ＬとＲの発音

日本人にとって、英語のＬとＲの発音は区別が難しいと言われています。必ずしも完璧である必要はありませんが、違いがわかるとリスニング力が高まりますし、相手にも情報を正確に伝えられます。

Ｌの発音：舌を上の歯の根元につける。　　**Ｒの発音**：口の中のどこにも舌先をつけない。

道順を案内するときに右（right）左（left）はよく使うので、違いを確認しておきましょう。

Exercises

 31

● Look at the sentences below and circle the words that you hear. Then, practice saying the sentences, paying attention to the sounds /l/ and /r/.

以下の英文を見て、聞こえたほうを丸で囲みましょう。もう一度音声を聞いて正しい発音をチェックし、【l】と【r】に気をつけながら発音を練習しましょう。

1.　Turn (**light / right**) at the next traffic (**light / right**).

2.　They (**laid / raid**) the mat on the floor and looked at the (**clouds / crowds**).

3.　The violin (**player / prayer**) quietly (**played / prayed**) for a successful concert.

V ‖Focus on Function

take の使い方

"take" は日常的によく使う単語ですが、様々な意味があります。最初に覚える意味は「手に取る」ではないでしょうか。今回はそれ以外の「（乗り物に）乗る」と「（時間が）かかる」という意味をマスターしましょう。

例）She took an apple from a box.（彼女は箱の中からリンゴを取った）

　　You have to take a bus to get there.（そこへ行くにはバスに乗る必要があります）

　　It'll take about 15 minutes on foot.　（歩いて 15 分ほどかかるでしょう）

Exercises

● Translate the Japanese sentences below into English using *take*.

日本文に合うように、空欄に適切な語を入れて英文を完成させましょう。

1.　レオンは彼女の手を取るために前かがみになった。

　　Leon leaned forward to ＿＿＿＿＿＿＿ her ＿＿＿＿＿＿＿ .

2.　その仕事を終えるのに、彼は長い時間かかった。

　　It ＿＿＿＿＿＿＿ him a ＿＿＿＿＿＿＿ time to complete the work.

3.　グランド・セントラル駅から地下鉄に乗ってください。

　　Please ＿＿＿＿＿＿＿ the ＿＿＿＿＿＿＿ from Grand Central Station.

VI | Find out

● **Find out about your classmates. Ask three people the following questions.**

クラスメートに質問してみましょう。3人に聞いて、答えを書いてください。

	Partner 1	Partner 2	Partner 3
1. Where is the nearest supermarket to your home?			
2. Is there a good café near here?			
3. How do you come to school?			
4. How much money do you spend on travel every week?			
5. How often do you take a taxi?			
6. Do you prefer taking a bus or a train?			
7. Your question: _____?			

Useful Language

Questions
- Where is . . . ?
- Is/Are there . . . ?
- How do you/we get to . . . ?

Answers
- There is/are . . .
- You need to take . . .
- You can get there by . . .

Details
- Transportation: car / bus / bicycle / taxi / train / subway / ferry / streetcar / airplane / bullet train
- Directions: next to / in front of / behind / opposite / near / far / to the left of / to the right of / between / turn / take

Notes

「〜がある」を示すには "There is/are" を使います。表現したいものが単数形のときは There is、複数形の時は There are になります。There is a fountain in the park.（その公園には噴水があります）このように、後ろに in . . . を続けて場所を表現することができます。

UNIT 7

Are you hungry?
– Talking about Food

I | Vocabulary

● **Part 1:** Match the Japanese words (a~j) to the English words (1~10).

1～10 の語の意味として適切なものを a～j から選びましょう。

a. 苦い	b. 非常においしい	c. 酸っぱい	d. 塩辛い	e. 甘い
f. 風味のある	g. においがする	h. 香辛料のきいた	i. 味がする	j. ～に見える

1. _____ sweet 　　　　2. _____ sour 　　　　3. _____ salty
4. _____ bitter 　　　　5. _____ savory 　　　6. _____ spicy
7. _____ smell 　　　　8. _____ look 　　　　9. _____ taste
10. _____ delicious

● **Part 2:** Complete the dialogs with words from Part 1.

Part 1 の単語リストから適切な語を選んで文を完成させましょう。

1. **A:** Are you okay? You look hot.
   B: Sorry. This curry is too _____ for me.

2. **A:** This is Japanese sushi.
   B: Wow! It _____ beautiful and tasty.

3. **A:** Fresh coffee _____ so good!
   B: Yes, it does. It tastes great, too!

4. **A:** What's your favorite food?
   B: It's New York style pizza. It's _____!

5. **A:** Do you like ice cream?
   B: Yes, I do. I love _____ foods.

🔵 **Listening Practice 1:** Listen to the conversation and check (✔) the boxes next to the sentences you hear.

会話を聞いて、どちらの表現が使われているか選んでチェックを入れましょう。

Speaker A	Speaker B
Hi, Kay.	
	Hey, Jō! What's that? ☐
	Hi, Jō! What are you eating? ☐
☐ This is a *nikuman*.	
☐ It's an *onigiri*.	
	I don't know what a *nikuman* is. ☐
	What is an *onigiri*? ☐
☐ A *nikuman* is a Chinese steamed bun.	
☐ It's a rice ball. It's rice wrapped in seaweed.	
	Is that it? It doesn't sound good. ☐
	Is that all? It doesn't sound tasty. ☐
☐ No. The bun is filled with meat.	
☐ No. There are many kinds of fillings.	
	Can I try one?
☐ Sure. Here you are.	
☐ Of course. Here you are.	
	Wow! It's so delicious! ☐
	It's so sour! I hate *umeboshi*! ☐

🔵 **Speaking Practice:** Practice the conversation with your partner.

パートナーと会話の練習をしましょう。

 33, 34

🔵 **Listening Practice 2:** Listen to two people talking about what they ate for a meal today. Write the meals and check (✔) the correct box for each item.

2人が今日の食事で何を食べたか話しているのを聞きましょう。朝食、昼食、夕食のどれについて話しているかを記入し、各項目について Yes か No を選びましょう。

1. Meal: _____

	Yes	No
sandwich	✔	☐
apple	☐	☐
coffee	☐	☐
green tea	☐	☐

2. Meal: _____

	Yes	No
sandwich	☐	☐
orange	☐	☐
coffee	☐	☐
green tea	☐	☐

III ‖ Conversation

 35

● **Part 1-1 (Get the gist):** Listen to the conversation and choose the correct answers (a~d).

会話を聞いて、最も適切なものを a ～ d の中から選びましょう。

1. Who are Mark and Sally most likely?
　　a. Friends
　　b. Brother and sister
　　c. Teacher and student
　　d. Restaurant worker and customer

2. What are they mainly talking about?
　　a. The food Sally likes most
　　b. The food Mark likes most
　　c. The food they both like
　　d. The food they will have for lunch

● **Part 1-2 (Get the details):** Listen to the conversation again and choose the correct answers (a~d).

もう一度会話を聞いて、最も適切なものを a ～ d の中から選びましょう。

3. What kind of food does Sally like best?
　　a. Spicy food
　　b. Salty food
　　c. Sweet food
　　d. Sour food

4. What is Mark's favorite food?
　　a. Miso soup
　　b. Sashimi
　　c. Wasabi
　　d. Green tea ice cream

● **Part 2:** Listen to the conversation again and write the missing words or phrases in the spaces.

会話をもう一度聞いて、空欄に適語を書き入れましょう。

Mark: Do you like (1) _____ food?

Sally: Yes, I do. I eat it nearly every day. I think it's delicious.

Mark: Really? I think so, too. What's your (2) _____?

Sally: What do you think it is, Mark?

Mark: That's such a difficult question, Sally! Hmm! Is it miso soup?

Sally: No. I like it, (3) _____ _____ it's too salty.

Mark: I see. Is it sashimi?

Sally: No. I like fish, but wasabi is too (4) _____ for me.

Mark: This is too hard. I need a hint. Is it sweet or (5) _____?

Sally: Oh, it's a sweet food. I love all sweet foods. I can't stand anything bitter, though.

Mark: I know what it is! It's green tea ice cream, isn't it?

Sally: Yes, (6) _____ _____!

Mark: That's my favorite, too! Let's go have some now. All that guessing has made me hungry!

● **Speaking Practice:** Practice the conversation with your partner.

パートナーと一緒に会話を練習しましょう。

40

IV ‖Pronunciation Check

イントネーションの違い

英語を話すとき、文末が上がったり下がったりします。基本的に以下のパターンがあるので覚えておきましょう。

例）I love all spicy food. ↘ ［通常の文章］

Do you like Chinese food? ↗ ［Yes/No を尋ねる疑問文］

What is your favorite sport? ↘ ［疑問詞で始まる疑問文］

Is it a vegetable (↗) or a fruit? (↘) ［二者択一で尋ねる文章。最初は上がり、次は下がります］

Exercises

 36

● **Listen to the recording and mark the correct intonation using ↗ or ↘ in the sentences below. Then, practice saying the sentences, paying attention to intonation.**

音声を聞いて、正しいイントネーションを矢印で示しましょう。もう一度音声を聞いて解答を確認した後、イントネーションに注意しながら、文章を読んで練習しましょう。

1. Did you see Andrew yesterday?

2. How does this soup taste?

3. Which do you like better, cats or dogs?

V ‖Focus on Function

〜 , isn't it? 「〜だよね？」

自分の話していることについて、相手の同意や確認を得たいときに付加疑問文を使います。イントネーションは、自分が確信を持っているときは下がり、あまり確信がなく相手に返答を求めるときは上がります。

例）It is warm today, isn't it?（今日は暖かいね）

He won the game, didn't he?（彼は試合に勝ったんだね）

上手に使って、スムーズなコミュニケーションをとれるようになりましょう。

Exercises

● **Complete the sentences with the correct question tag.**

次の文章を付加疑問文にしてみましょう。

1. She is going to buy a guitar, _____ _____?

2. Nathan speaks Japanese well, _____ _____?

3. You will see him tomorrow, _____ _____?

VI Find out

● **Find out about your classmates. Ask three people the following questions.**

クラスメートに質問してみましょう。3人に聞いて、答えを書いてください。

	Partner 1	Partner 2	Partner 3
1. Do you like spicy food?			
2. Which do you like better, sweet or savory food?			
3. What's your favorite food?			
4. What's your favorite drink?			
5. Have you ever tried _____?			
6. Have you ever eaten _____?			
7. Your question: _____?			

Note: savory：「風味のある」以外に、「辛口の、塩味の効いた」という意味もある。

Useful Language

Questions

- Do you . . . ?
- Which do you like better, . . . or . . . ?
- Have you ever . . . ?

Answers

- Yes, I do. / No, I don't.
- I like . . . better.
- Yes, I have. / No, I haven't.

Details

- Food: green pepper / cheese / eggplant / pasta / natto
- Adjectives: slimy / smelly / sweet / sour / sharp / salty / bitter / (un)healthy / junky / oily / greasy / savory / salty
- Verbs: look / smell / taste

Notes

現在完了形（have ＋過去分詞）を使って、これまでの**経験**を表現することができます。Have you ever . . . ？と尋ねられたら、Yes, I have. または No, I haven't. と答えましょう。主語が he/she/it など三人称単数のときは have が has になります。

UNIT 8

Let's eat!
– Talking about Restaurants and Meals

I Vocabulary

● **Part 1:** Match the Japanese words (a~j) to the English words (1~10).

1～10 の語の意味として適切なものを a～j から選びましょう。

a. 注文する	b. 夕食	c. デザート	d. 昼食	e. 空腹な
f. 朝食	g. 抜かす	h. 予約	i. 決定する	j. アレルギーの

1. _____ hungry   2. _____ skip   3. _____ reservation

4. _____ allergic   5. _____ order   6. _____ dessert

7. _____ breakfast   8. _____ lunch   9. _____ dinner

10. _____ decide

● **Part 2:** Complete the dialogs with words from Part 1.

Part 1 の単語リストから適切な語を選んで文を完成させましょう。

1. **A:** Is there any food you can't eat?

   B: Yes, there is. I'm _____ to nuts.

2. **A:** Can I help you?

   B: Yes, I'd like to _____ a pizza, please.

3. **A:** Do you think we need a(n) _____?

   B: Yes, I do. It's a very popular restaurant.

4. **A:** Do you ever _____ breakfast?

   B: Sometimes I do. But, only when I'm late for school.

5. **A:** What did you have for _____ last night?

   B: I had sushi.

43

● **Listening Practice 1:** Listen to the conversation and check (✔) the boxes next to the sentences you hear.

会話を聞いて、どちらの表現が使われているか選んでチェックを入れましょう。

Speaker A	Speaker B
☐ I'm hungry!	
☐ Wow, it's already 12:30.	
	Okay, let's eat. ☐
	Shall we have lunch? ☐
☐ Good idea. Where shall we go?	
☐ That's a good idea. What shall we have?	
	Let me see. There's a Thai restaurant . . . ☐
	How about a hamburger? ☐
☐ I don't feel like eating a burger.	
☐ Thai food is too spicy for me.	
	I see. Is sushi okay? ☐
	Really? How about ramen? ☐
☐ Ramen would be great.	
☐ Sushi sounds good.	
	Then it's decided. Let's go. ☐
	Sushi it is! Let's go. ☐
Great! I'm really hungry.	
	Me, too. I skipped breakfast.

● **Speaking Practice:** Practice the conversation with your partner.

パートナーと会話を練習しましょう。

 38, 39

● **Listening Practice 2:** Listen to two people talking about their favorite food. Write the foods and check (✔) the correct box for each item.

2人が好きな食べ物について話しているのを聞きましょう。食べ物を記入し、それぞれの情報について Yes か No を選びましょう。

1. Food: _____

	Yes	No
likes Lala Pizza	☐	☐
goes two times a week	☐	☐
always orders seafood pizza	☐	☐
is allergic to shrimp	☐	☐

2. Food: _____

	Yes	No
likes GoGo Sushi	☐	☐
goes five times a week	☐	☐
always orders *tamagozushi*	☐	☐
is allergic to seafood	☐	☐

III ‖Conversation

 40

● **Part 1-1 (Get the gist):** Listen to the conversation and choose the correct answers (a~d).

会話を聞いて、最も適切なものを a ～ d の中から選びましょう。

1. Who most likely made the reservation?
   a. Mayumi
   b. Yuriko
   c. The waiter
   d. The restaurant

2. What kind of meal will they probably eat?
   a. Breakfast
   b. Lunch
   c. Dinner
   d. Picnic

● **Part 1-2 (Get the details):** Listen to the conversation again and choose the correct answers (a~d).

もう一度会話を聞いて、最も適切なものを a ～ d の中から選びましょう。

3. How many people order the afternoon tea set?
   a. 1
   b. 2
   c. 3
   d. 4

4. Which of the following is correct?
   a. Mayumi does not like eggs.
   b. Yuriko does not like eggs.
   c. Mayumi cannot eat eggs.
   d. Yuriko cannot eat eggs.

5. What will the waiter bring first?
   a. Tea
   b. Champagne
   c. Sandwiches
   d. Scones

● **Part 2:** Listen to the conversation again and write the missing words or phrases in the spaces.

会話をもう一度聞いて、空欄に適語を書き入れましょう。

Waiter: Good afternoon.

Mayumi: Hello. A table for two, please. We have a (1) _____ for Yamada Mayumi.

Waiter: Thank you. Please come this way.

〈**A short time later**〉

Waiter: Are you (2) _____ _____ _____?

Mayumi: I can't decide. It all (3) _____ _____ _____. What do you want, Yuriko?

Yuriko: I'm not sure. Excuse me. Can you (4) _____ me what the afternoon tea set is, please?

Waiter: (5) _____. The afternoon tea set is two kinds of sandwich, cucumber and egg, scones with strawberry jam and cream, four kinds of cake, tea, and a glass of champagne.

Yuriko: That sounds like a picnic! I'll have that, please. (6) _____ _____ _____, Mayumi?

Mayumi: I'll have that, too. But, no egg sandwiches for me, please. I'm (7) _____ to eggs.

Waiter: So, that's two afternoon tea sets, one with no egg sandwiches. Thank you very much. I'll bring your champagne right away.

● **Speaking Practice:** Practice the conversation with your partner.

パートナーと一緒に会話を練習しましょう。

IV Pronunciation Check

アクセントの位置 -tion / -sion

英語にはアクセントのルールがあります。アクセントは母音につけますが、単語によっては母音がいくつか入っています。そのような場合、正しい位置にアクセントがつけられると、情報が正確に伝わります。接尾辞が -tion や -sion などの語は、その直前にアクセントを置くので覚えておきましょう。

例）reservation［-tion の直前の母音 a にアクセントを置く］
　　＊例外　television は -sion の直前ではなく、最初の e にアクセントを置きます。

Exercises

 41

● **Listen to the recording and choose the correct stress pattern for the underlined words in the sentences below. Then, practice saying the sentences, paying attention to stress.**

音声を聞いて、正しいアクセントに下線が引いてあるものを選びましょう。もう一度音声を聞いて解答を確認した後、強弱に注意しながら発音の練習をしましょう。

1. Where will you go on vacation?

   a. vacation　　　　b. vacation　　　　c. vacation

2. I think that the decision was correct.

   a. decision　　　　b. decision　　　　c. decision

3. The pronunciation of this word is very difficult for me.

   a. pronunciation　　b. pronunciation　　c. pronunciation

V Focus on Function

kind of . . . 種類を示す

種類やタイプを表すときに名詞の "kind" を使います。前置詞 of の後ろに種類を示したいものを加えます。"a kind of . . ."「〜の一種」や "three kinds of . . ."「3 種類の〜」のように、kind の前に数字を示します。複数の場合は、kinds になるので注意しましょう。"a kind of . . ." は、「ある種の〜、〜のようなもの」という意味でも使います。

例）two kinds of sandwich（2 種類のサンドイッチ）
　　a kind of flower（花の一種）

Exercises

● **Translate the Japanese sentences below into English using *kind of*.**

日本文に合うように、適切な語を入れて英文を完成させましょう。

1. その店では、6 種類のピザを売っている。

   They sell ＿＿＿＿＿＿＿ ＿＿＿＿＿＿＿ ＿＿＿＿＿＿＿ pizza at the store.

2. 彼は一種の副業を始めた。

   He started ＿＿＿＿＿＿＿ ＿＿＿＿＿＿＿ ＿＿＿＿＿＿＿ side business.

3. どんな種類の音楽が好きですか?

   What ＿＿＿＿＿＿＿ ＿＿＿＿＿＿＿ ＿＿＿＿＿＿＿ do you like?

VI ‖ Find out

● **Find out about your classmates. Ask three people the following questions.**

クラスメートに質問してみましょう。3人に聞いて、答えを書いてください。

	Partner 1	Partner 2	Partner 3
1. Which do you prefer, eating out or eating at home?			
2. How often do you eat out?			
3. What's your favorite restaurant?			
4. What's your favorite dish?			
5. When did you last eat out?			
6. Are you allergic to anything?			
7. Your question: _____?			

Useful Language

Questions
- Which do you . . . ?
- What's your favorite . . . ?
- Are you allergic to . . . ?

Answers
- I like . . .
- My favorite . . . is . . .
- I'm allergic to . . .

Details
- Kinds of restaurant: French / Chinese / Italian / Japanese / Spanish / Mexican / Hawaiian / Vietnamese / Thai / Turkish / Korean / fast food / family
- Restaurant language: reserve / reservation / order / choose / decide / table
- Talking about food and meals: breakfast / lunch / dinner / dessert / snack / hungry / skip / allergic / buffet

Notes

「～のアレルギーがある」は "I'm allergic to . . ." という表現を使います。相手に質問する場合は、"Are you allergic to . . . ?"「～にアレルギーはありますか?」または "Do you have any allergies?"「何かアレルギーはありますか?」と尋ねます。

UNIT 9

What are you watching?
– Talking about Movies and TV

I ｜ Vocabulary

● **Part 1:** Match the Japanese words (a~j) to the English words and phrases (1~10).

1～10 の語の意味として適切なものを a ～ j から選びましょう。

a. 映画	b. 喜劇	c. 監督	d. サイエンス・フィクション映画	e. 恋愛
f. 続き物	g. 俳優	h. 番組	i. 著名人	j. 劇場

1. ____ movie   2. ____ theater   3. ____ actor

4. ____ director   5. ____ series   6. ____ romance

7. ____ program   8. ____ celebrity   9. ____ comedy

10. ____ science fiction

● **Part 2:** Complete the dialogs with words and phrases from Part 1.

Part 1 の単語リストから適切な語を選んで文を完成させましょう。

1. **A:** Do you prefer watching movies at home or at the movie _____?
   B: Definitely at home.

2. **A:** What's your favorite type of movie?
   B: I'd have to say _____. I love movies that make me laugh.

3. **A:** Do you like movies with _____ in them?
   B: Not really. I think love stories are boring.

4. **A:** Do you like _____ movies?
   B: No, I prefer true stories and documentaries about real people.

5. **A:** Do you have a favorite TV _____?
   B: Yes, I like watching Music Station the most.

● **Listening Practice 1:** Listen to the conversation and check (✔) the boxes next to the sentences you hear.

会話を聞いて、どちらの表現が使われているか選んでチェックを入れましょう。

Speaker A	Speaker B
☐ Do you want to watch a movie this weekend? ☐ Would you like to watch a movie this weekend?	
	Yes, sure. Which one? ☐ Yes, nice idea. Which one? ☐
☐ There's a horror movie I'd like to watch. ☐ There's a romance movie I'd like to watch.	
	I prefer action movies. ☐ I like action movies better. ☐
OK, let's watch an action movie then.	Do you mean at the theater? ☐ At the theater, right? ☐
☐ Yes, it's more exciting. ☐ Yes, it's more interesting.	
	I agree. When shall we go? ☐ I think so, too. When shall we go? ☐
☐ How about Saturday evening? ☐ Are you free on Saturday evening?	
	Yes, let's go then. ☐ Sounds great! ☐

● **Speaking Practice:** Practice the conversation with your partner.

パートナーと会話を練習しましょう。

 43, 44

● **Listening Practice 2:** Listen to two people talking about movies they saw recently. Write the types of movie and check (✔) the correct box for each item.

最近観た映画について、2人が話しているのを聞きましょう。映画のタイプを記入し、それぞれの情報について Yes か No を選びましょう。

1. Type of movie: _____

	Yes	No
watched it at home	☐	☐
watched it alone	☐	☐
liked it	☐	☐
will watch it again	☐	☐

2. Type of movie: _____

	Yes	No
watched it at home	☐	☐
watched it alone	☐	☐
liked it	☐	☐
will watch it again	☐	☐

III ‖Conversation

 45

● **Part 1-1 (Get the gist):** Listen to the conversation and choose the correct answers (a~d).

会話を聞いて、最も適切なものを a〜d の中から選びましょう。

1. What can we infer about Peter and Jasmine?
   a. They are brother and sister.
   b. They are classmates.
   c. They live together.
   d. They love all kinds of TV programs.

2. How does Jasmine probably feel about the programs on TV tonight?
   a. Tired   **b.** Scared
   c. Excited   **d.** Uninterested

● **Part 1-2 (Get the details):** Listen to the conversation again and choose the correct answers (a~d).

もう一度会話を聞いて、最も適切なものを a〜d の中から選びましょう。

3. What channel is the news on?
   a. Channel 1
   b. Channel 2
   c. Channel 3
   d. Channel 4

4. Who likes the science fiction series?
   a. Peter
   b. Peter's friends
   c. Jasmine
   d. Jasmine's friends

5. What does Jasmine want to watch?
   a. A horror movie
   b. The news
   c. A rugby match
   d. A comedy program

● **Part 2:** Listen to the conversation again and write the missing words or phrases in the spaces.

会話をもう一度聞いて、空欄に適語を書き入れましょう。

Peter: I'm tired, Jasmine, I don't want to go out tonight. Let's just

(1) _____ _____ and watch TV.

Jasmine: That sounds like a good plan, Peter. I don't want to go out either.

Peter: OK, (2) _____ _____ _____ at the TV

guide. So, there's a horror movie on Channel 1, a rugby match on

Channel 2, news on Channel 3, and the new science fiction series on

Channel 4.

Jasmine: Oh, (3) _____ not rugby. I don't understand the rules. Is the

science fiction series good?

Peter: I don't know, but my friends like it. The horror movie looks good. It was

made by a famous director.

Jasmine: (4) _____ _____ _____?

Peter: Umm . . . It's about zombies attacking a (5) _____ mall.

Jasmine: Oh no, that doesn't sound like fun at all. Isn't there any comedy on?

That would be good.

Peter: No, there isn't. Watching the news all (6) _____ doesn't sound

like fun, does it?

Jasmine: No! Let's go out.

Peter: Yes, I think that might be (7) _____.

● **Speaking Practice:** Practice the conversation with your partner.

パートナーと一緒に会話を練習しましょう。

IV Pronunciation Check

消える音／副詞 (-ly) の前の t

ネイティブスピーカーの発音を聞くと、スペルにあっても聞こえない音があります。そのような音が消える現象を Reduction（リダクション）と呼びます。その一つが、副詞 (-ly) の前にある t の音です。消えている音を意識するとリスニング力がアップしますし、話すときも意識してみると発音が上達します。

例）exactly → exac(t)ly のように聞こえます。

Exercises

 46

🔵 **Listen to the recording and choose the sentence which uses reduction, A or B. Then, practice saying the sentences, paying attention to reduction.**

音声を聞いて、リダクションが起きているものを選びましょう。その後、リダクションに注意しながら発音を練習してみましょう。

1. Honestly, I can't believe it.   A   B

2. She will definitely come today.   A   B

3. Miguel hasn't had any time to study recently.   A   B

V Focus on Function

sound like . . . 「〜のようだね」

相手の話に対して、「〜のようだね、〜そうだね」と相槌を打つ場合、"sound like" の表現が便利です。like の後ろには名詞が続きます。相手の話の内容を That で示して、「それは〜そうだね」という言い方がよく使われますが、主語が単数の場合は sounds と 3 人称単数の s が付くので注意しましょう。

例）That sounds like a good plan.（それは良い計画のようだね）

Exercises

🔵 **Translate the Japanese sentences below into English using *sound like*.**

日本文に合うように、空欄に適切な語を入れて英文を完成させましょう。

1. **A:** I'm planning to celebrate my grandmother's birthday this weekend.
   B: That _____ _____ a _____ _____ .
   （それは良い考えだね。）

2. **A:** He told me the same story three times!
   B: That doesn't _____ _____ _____ at all.
   （それは全く楽しくなさそう。）

3. **A:** He proposed to Sophia on a luxury cruise ship.
   B: It _____ _____ _____ _____ .
   （それは映画みたいだね。）

VI | Find out

● **Find out about your classmates. Ask three people the following questions.**

クラスメートに質問してみましょう。3人に聞いて、答えを書いてください。

	Partner 1	Partner 2	Partner 3
1. How often do you watch TV?			
2. What's your favorite TV program?			
3. What's a kind of TV program you don't like?			
4. Do you prefer watching TV or videos online?			
5. How often do you go to the movie theater?			
6. Who's your favorite actor or TV celebrity?			
7. Your question: _____?			

Useful Language

Questions
- How often do you . . . ?
- What's your favorite . . . ?
- Do you prefer . . . ?

Answers
- I . . . every day/once a week.
- My favorite . . . is/are . . .
- I prefer . . .

Details
- Genres: comedy / action / horror / mystery / romance / science fiction / fantasy / historical drama / documentary / drama

Notes

「どれくらい〜しますか？」と頻度を尋ねる時は "How often . . . ?" を使います。How often do you . . . ? How often does he . . . ? のように、後ろに一般動詞の疑問文を続けます。答える時は every day「毎日」、once a week「週に1回」、about three times a month「月に3回くらい」などの表現を使いましょう。

54

UNIT 10

What music do you like?
– Talking about Music

I │ Vocabulary

● **Part 1: Match the Japanese words (a~j) to the English words (1~10).**
1 〜 10 の語の意味として適切なものを a 〜 j から選びましょう。

a. グループ	b. アイドル	c. 道具・楽器	d. 様式	e. 踊る
f. 声	g. 古典の	h. 芸術家	i. 組み合わせ	j. 演奏会

1. ____ instrument   2. ____ combination   3. ____ voice

4. ____ concert   5. ____ dance   6. ____ group

7. ____ classical   8. ____ idol   9. ____ artist

10. ____ genre

● **Part 2: Complete the dialogs with words from Part 1.**
Part 1 の単語リストから適切な語を選んで文を完成させましょう。

1. **A:** Have you ever been to a live _____?
   B: No, but I really want to see my favorite singer perform live next month.

2. **A:** Do you like K-pop?
   B: Yes, I love it! The artists can sing and _____ so well.

3. **A:** Can you play a musical _____?
   B: No. I tried to learn when I was younger, but it was too difficult.

4. **A:** Do you like karaoke?
   B: I like it, but I can't sing well. My _____ is awful!

5. **A:** Is there any music you don't like?
   B: No, not really. I like every _____ of music.

● **Listening Practice 1:** Listen to the conversation and check (✔) the boxes next to the sentences you hear.

会話を聞いて、どちらの表現が使われているか選んでチェックを入れましょう。

Speaker A	Speaker B
Hi, Lucy. What are you listening to?	
	☐ Hi. It's my favorite J-pop artist.
	☐ Hi. It's my favorite K-pop artist.
☐ Nice! I like that genre, too.	
☐ Nice! Who is your favorite artist?	
	☐ It's great, isn't it?
	☐ It's GReeeeN. Do you know them?
Yes. So, do you like karaoke?	
	☐ I love it! How about you?
	☐ Not so much. How about you?
☐ Yes, but I don't have a good voice.	
☐ Yes. My friends say I'm a good singer.	
	☐ Great! I'd like to hear you sing!
	☐ It doesn't matter. You should still sing!
☐ Shall we go to karaoke together?	
☐ Let's sing at karaoke together.	
	☐ Yes, let's do that.
	☐ Umm . . . OK. Let's go.

● **Speaking Practice:** Practice the conversation with your partner.

パートナーと会話を練習しましょう。

🎧 48, 49

● **Listening Practice 2:** Listen to two people talking about musical instruments they play. Write the instruments and check (✔) the correct box for each item.

2人が演奏する楽器について話しているのを聞きましょう。楽器を記入し、それぞれの情報について Yes か No を選びましょう。

1. Instrument: _____

	Yes	No
plays alone	☐	☐
takes lessons	☐	☐
plays well	☐	☐
has their own instrument	☐	☐

2. Instrument: _____

	Yes	No
plays alone	☐	☐
takes lessons	☐	☐
plays well	☐	☐
has their own instrument	☐	☐

III ‖Conversation ● 50

● **Part 1-1 (Get the gist):** Listen to the conversation and choose the correct answers (a~d).

会話を聞いて、最も適切なものを a ～ d の中から選びましょう。

1. How does Yumi feel about going to the concert?
   - **a.** Excited
   - **b.** Surprised
   - **c.** Bored
   - **d.** Scared

2. What can we infer about Tom and Yumi?
   - **a.** They both like idol groups.
   - **b.** They like different kinds of music.
   - **c.** They are both cute and dance really well.
   - **d.** They are going to a concert together.

● **Part 1-2 (Get the details):** Listen to the conversation again and choose the correct answers (a~d).

もう一度会話を聞いて、最も適切なものを a ～ d の中から選びましょう。

3. Who will perform at the concert this weekend?
   - **a.** Tom
   - **b.** Yumi
   - **c.** Idol groups
   - **d.** Rock groups

4. What does Tom say he has never done?
   - **a.** Been to a live concert
   - **b.** Seen idol groups on TV
   - **c.** Seen idol groups live
   - **d.** Seen many different artists

5. Why does Tom say he likes rock groups?
   - **a.** Because they play live concerts.
   - **b.** Because they are cute.
   - **c.** Because they dance well.
   - **d.** Because they have good energy.

Part 2: Listen to the conversation again and write the missing words or phrases in the spaces.

会話をもう一度聞いて、空欄に適語を書き入れましょう。

Tom: What are you doing (1) _____ _____, Yumi?

Yumi: I'm going to a concert. I can't wait!

Tom: Wow, that's (2)_____! I'm really jealous! Whose concert is it?

Yumi: It's a combination of different idol groups. They're all so cute and dance really well.

Tom: I've (3) _____ some idol groups on TV, but never live. Who's your favorite?

Yumi: It's a difficult choice, I (4) _____ _____ _____! No, I can't decide.

Tom: Maybe it's best that there will be lots of (5) _____ artists and groups at the concert then.

Yumi: Yes, (6) _____ _____ _____ right. What music do you like, Tom?

Tom: I like rock. I love the good (7) _____ rock groups have.

Yumi: Rock? Wow, very different from idol music!

Speaking Practice: Practice the conversation with your partner.

パートナーと一緒に会話を練習しましょう。

IV Pronunciation Check

つながる音　n＋母音

Unit 4 では英語のつながる音「t＋母音」について学びました。その他にもつながる音として「n＋母音」の形があります。アルファベットの n で終わる単語の次に母音で始まる単語が続くとき、音がつながって聞こえます。話すときにも意識して発音してみましょう。

例）It's a combination of different idol groups.［下線部の箇所がつなげて発音されます］

Exercises
 51

● **Listen to the recording and connect the linked words using ⌣ in the sentences below. Then, practice saying the sentences, paying attention to linking.**

音声を聞いて、つながる音に印 (⌣) を付けましょう。その後、つながる音に注意して発音を練習してみましょう。

1. Jan, answer the question as soon as possible.

2. Can you turn out the light when leaving the room?

3. Don't turn the television on now, it's time for bed.

V Focus on Function

Whose 誰のもの？

誰のものかを尋ねるときは、疑問詞の "whose" を使います。「これは誰の〜？」という場合、"Whose bag is this?"「これは誰のバッグですか？」のように whose の後ろに名詞を続けて、is/are などの be 動詞を用いた疑問文の形になります。もう一つの尋ね方として、「この〜は誰のものですか？」と聞く場合には、"Whose is this bag?"「このバッグは誰のものですか？」のように、whose の後ろに be 動詞を続けます。また、物以外に人に対しても使うことができます。

例）Whose father is he?（彼は誰のお父さんなの？）

Exercises

● **Translate the Japanese sentences below into English using *whose*.**

日本文に合うように whose を使って英文を完成させましょう。

1. この本は誰のものですか？

   ＿＿＿＿＿＿＿＿＿ ＿＿＿＿＿＿＿＿＿ this ＿＿＿＿＿＿＿＿ ?

2. 誰の絵が一番良かったですか？

   ＿＿＿＿＿＿＿＿＿ ＿＿＿＿＿＿＿＿＿ was the best?

3. これは誰の帽子 (hat) かわからない。

   I don't ＿＿＿＿＿＿＿＿ ＿＿＿＿＿＿＿＿＿ ＿＿＿＿＿＿＿＿ this is.

VI │ Find out

● **Find out about your classmates. Ask three people the following questions.**

クラスメートに質問してみましょう。3 人に聞いて、答えを書いてください。

	Partner 1	Partner 2	Partner 3
1. What's your favorite type of music?			
2. What's a type of music you dislike?			
3. Can you play a musical instrument?			
4. Have you ever been to a live concert?			
5. Which do you prefer, pop music or classical music?			
6. Do you like karaoke?			
7. Your question: _____?			

Useful Language

Questions
- What's a type of . . . you like / dislike?
- Can you . . . ?
- Have you ever been to . . . ?

Answers
- I like / don't like . . .
- Yes, I can. / No, I can't.
- Yes, I have. / No, I haven't.

Details
- Genres: rock / jazz / country / hip hop / blues / folk / R&B / dance / soul / reggae / rap / heavy metal

Notes

「～を演奏する」という場合、基本的に
楽器には定冠詞 the を付けます。
例) She can play the piano.
楽器を買う、作る、などの時は the を
付ける必要はないので区別しましょう。
例) He bought a guitar yesterday.
　　My father makes violins.

UNIT 11

How much is it?
– Talking about Shopping

I Vocabulary

● **Part 1:** Match the Japanese words (a~j) to the English words and phrases (1~10).
1 ～ 10 の語の意味として適切なものを a ～ j から選びましょう。

a. 一対の	b. 試着する	c. 現金	d. 合う	e. きつい
f. 束・房	g. 緩い	h. 大きさ	i. 袋・箱	j. 必要とする

1. ____ cash   2. ____ try (something) on   3. ____ loose
4. ____ tight   5. ____ a pair of   6. ____ size
7. ____ bunch   8. ____ packet   9. ____ fit
10. ____ need

● **Part 2:** Complete the dialogs with words and phrases from Part 1.
Part 1 の単語リストから適切な語を選んで文を完成させましょう。

1. **A:** That's a really big ice cream, isn't it?
   B: Yes, it is. I always order the extra-large _____.

2. **A:** What's wrong?
   B: I ate too much in the winter vacation. Now my pants are too
   _____.

3. **A:** I love this jacket. It's so cool!
   B: Will it _____ you? It looks too small. You should try it on.

4. **A:** I have to go to the bank and get some _____.
   B: Don't worry. I can lend you some money.

5. **A:** I really want to buy that red pair of shoes.
   B: You have lots of shoes. You don't _____ a new pair.

II Warm-up for Listening & Speaking

 EC CD 52

● Listening Practice 1: Listen to the conversation and check (✔) the boxes next to the sentences you hear.

会話を聞いて、どちらの表現が使われているか選んでチェックを入れましょう。

Speaker A	Speaker B
Can I help you?	
	☐ Yes, please. Can I try these jeans on?
	☐ Yes, please. Do you have this hair band in blue?
☐ I'll go and check . . . I'm sorry, we don't.	
☐ Sure. The fitting rooms are at the back of the shop on the left.	
	☐ Oh, thanks anyway.
	☐ Thanks.
☐ How are they?	
☐ Can I help you with anything else?	
	☐ Yes, can I see that blue belt?
	☐ They're a little tight. Do you have a medium pair?
☐ Yes, we do. Here you are.	
☐ Certainly. Here you are.	
	☐ These fit just fine. I'll take them. How much are they?
	☐ It's really nice. How much is it?
6,500 yen. Will you pay by cash or credit card?	
	Cash, please. Here you are.

● Speaking Practice: Practice the conversation with your partner.

パートナーと会話を練習しましょう。

CD 53, 54

● Listening Practice 2: Listen to two people talking about places they went shopping. Write the places and check (✔) the correct box for each item.

2 人が買い物について話しているのを聞きましょう。買い物をした場所を記入し、それぞれの情報について Yes か No を選びましょう。

1. Place: _____

	Yes	No
likes shopping	☐	☐
visited 2 shops	☐	☐
bought a hat	☐	☐
spent ¥50,000	☐	☐

2. Place: _____

	Yes	No
likes shopping	☐	☐
visited 2 shops	☐	☐
bought a computer	☐	☐
spent ¥50,000	☐	☐

III ‖Conversation

 55

● **Part 1-1 (Get the gist):** Listen to the conversation and choose the correct answers (a~d).

会話を聞いて、最も適切なものを a ～ d の中から選びましょう。

1. Where are Ami and Bimal most likely talking?
    a. At work
    b. At school
    c. At home
    d. At a shopping mall

2. What will they probably do next?
    a. Use the internet
    b. Wait for their shopping
    c. Have lunch together
    d. Go to a supermarket

● **Part 1-2 (Get the details):** Listen to the conversation again and choose the correct answers (a~d).

もう一度会話を聞いて、最も適切なものを a ～ d の中から選びましょう。

3. Which of the following foods does Bimal <u>not</u> suggest?
    a. Apples
    b. Bananas
    c. Cornflakes
    d. Rice

4. How much will they pay for their shopping?
    a. $5.00
    b. $40.65
    c. $45.65
    d. $50.00

5. What does Bimal think about online shopping?
    a. It is expensive.
    b. It is convenient.
    c. It is difficult.
    d. It is really bad.

55

Part 2: Listen to the conversation again and write the missing words or phrases in the spaces.

会話をもう一度聞いて、空欄に適語を書き入れましょう。

Ami: Bimal, we need to do some shopping for groceries.

Bimal: What? But the (1) _____ is really bad today, Ami.

Ami: Don't worry. We'll buy everything online and (2) _____ _____ _____. But I'm not sure what we need to buy. Can you go to the (3) _____ and tell me?

Bimal: Sure. Well, we need some rice and cornflakes.

Ami: A (4) _____ _____ _____ rice, and a box of cornflakes. Got it. Is there anything else?

Bimal: Yes, there is. We should get some tea and coffee. Can you order some cookies, too? Oh, and some milk and bananas.

Ami: Okay. One box of teabags, a jar of coffee, a packet of cookies, a (5) _____ of milk, and a bunch of bananas. I'll get some apples, too. Is that all?

Bimal: Yes, that's everything. (6) _____ _____ _____ _____?

Ami: That comes to $40.65. With a same-day delivery charge of $5, the total is (7) _____. That's not so expensive, less than $50.

Bimal: That was easy. We should shop online every time.

Speaking Practice: Practice the conversation with your partner.

パートナーと一緒に会話を練習しましょう。

IV ‖ Pronunciation Check

but, bud, bad, bat の発音

Unit 3 では see、sea、she の発音を学びました。その他にも、綴りが似ているけれども違う発音の単語があります。接続詞の but「しかし」は【bʌt】（カタカナのアを喉の奥から出すような音）と発音します。弱く発音する場合は、【bət】（口を狭く開けてアとウの中間のような音）としますが、ここでは前者の発音を覚えておきましょう。植物の蕾を表す語 bud も【bʌd】で、アに近い音です。それに対して、形容詞の bad「悪い」は【bæd】（口を横に広げてアとエを同時に出すような音）になります。野球などの「バット」bat も同じように【bæt】と発音します。

Exercises

 56

● Look at the sentences below and circle the words that you hear. Then, practice saying the sentences, paying attention to the sounds /ʌ/ and /æ/.

音声を聞いて、聞こえたほうを丸で囲みましょう。もう一度音声を聞いて正しい発音をチェックし、【ʌ】と【æ】に気をつけながら発音の練習をしましょう。

1. The man wearing the (**hat / hut**) appeared from the (**hat / hut**).
2. The (**but / bad / bud**) weather continued for a long time, (**but / bad / bud**) the rose (**but / bad / bud**) began to open up.
3. The boy caught many (**bags / bugs**) and put them into the plastic (**bags / bugs**).

V ‖ Focus on Function

a bunch of . . . 「一房（一束）の〜」

英語には、"a cup of tea" のように食料や飲料、物質の数量の表し方がいくつかあります。可算名詞で房や束になっているものは、"a bunch of . . ." を使います。
例）a bunch of bananas（一房のバナナ）
他にも、切り分けていない大きなケーキは a cake、two cakes と表現できますが、切り分けると数えられない名詞となり、a piece of cake または a slice of cake と表現します。瓶に入っているものは "a jar of . . ."、紙の容器や牛乳、ジュースなどのパックは "a carton of . . ." を使います。

Exercises

● Choose the correct word for each sentence.

日本文に合うように、適切な数量を表す表現を選びましょう。

1. 今朝はパンを一切れ食べた。
   I ate a (**bottle / slice / bunch**) of bread this morning.
2. エリカは叔母から一束のカギを預かった。
   Erika received a (**piece / carton / bunch**) of keys from her aunt.
3. その男の子は母親が作った1瓶のマーマレードを持ってきた。
   The boy brought a (**glass / jar / bunch**) of his mother's home-made marmalade.

VI │ Find out

● **Find out about your classmates. Ask three people the following questions.**

クラスメートに質問してみましょう。3人に聞いて、答えを書いてください。

	Partner 1	Partner 2	Partner 3
1. Do you like shopping?			
2. How often do you go shopping?			
3. Where do you like to shop?			
4. When did you last go shopping?			
5. What is the most expensive thing you have ever bought?			
6. Which do you prefer, online shopping or going to a shop?			
7. Your question: _____?			

Useful Language

Questions
- Do you like . . . ?
- How often do you . . . ?
- Where do you like to . . . ?

Answers
- Yes, I do. / No, I don't.
- I like to . . .

Details
- Quantifiers: a glass of / a cup of / a bottle of / a pot of / a piece of / a box of / a bag of / a head of / a pack of / a can of / a packet of / a pair of / a bunch of
- Clothes: try on / fit / loose / tight / big / small / size

Notes

値段について表現するとき、「高い」は "expensive" を使います。「安い」にはいくつか表現があり、"cheap" は値段が安いという意味ですが、安っぽい、質が劣る、というニュアンスがあります。"reasonable" は値段が手ごろ、"inexpensive" は値段があまり高くない、という表現になります。

UNIT 12

Let's play!
– Talking about Sports and Exercise

I Vocabulary

● **Part 1:** Match the Japanese words (a~j) to the English words (1~10).

1 ～ 10 の語の意味として適切なものを a ～ j から選びましょう。

| a. 勝ち抜き戦 | b. 体育館 | c. 個人の | d. 試合 | e. ラケット |
| f. 運動・競技 | g. 競争の | h. 滑って転ぶ | i. 監督・指導員 | j. 体操・運動 |

1. ____ exercise
2. ____ sport
3. ____ individual
4. ____ competitive
5. ____ tournament
6. ____ coach
7. ____ match
8. ____ racket
9. ____ gym
10. ____ slip

● **Part 2:** Complete the dialogs with words from Part 1.

Part 1 の単語リストから適切な語を選んで文を完成させましょう。

1. **A:** What's your favorite _____?
   B: I love basketball. It's so exciting!

2. **A:** How was the volleyball _____?
   B: We did well, but we lost in the final. Next time we'll win.

3. **A:** How often do you do sport or _____?
   B: Not often. I prefer to play computer games.

4. **A:** What's in your bag?
   B: It's my badminton _____. I've got practice tonight.

5. **A:** You've been practicing really hard recently.
   B: Yes, we've got a(n) _____ against a good team soon.

● **Listening Practice 1:** Listen to the conversation and check (✔) the boxes next to the sentences you hear.

会話を聞いて、どちらの表現が使われているか選んでチェックを入れましょう。

Speaker A	Speaker B
What happened to your arm?	
	I hurt it at judo practice. ☐
	I hurt it doing judo yesterday. ☐
☐ Oh no. What happened?	
☐ Oh dear. How?	
	I slipped and fell on it. ☐
	I fell badly on it. ☐
☐ Ouch! How often do you do judo?	
☐ Ouch! Do you do judo a lot?	
	Yes, at least three times a week. ☐
	At least three times a week. ☐
☐ I want to try judo, but I'm a bit scared.	
☐ I'd like to try it, but I'm a bit scared.	
	Don't be scared. It's safe and fun! ☐
	Don't worry! It's safe and fun! ☐
Safe? Look at your arm!	
	Oh, right. ☐
	That was me, not judo! ☐

● **Speaking Practice:** Practice the conversation with your partner.

パートナーと会話を練習しましょう。

🎧 **CD** 58, 59

● **Listening Practice 2:** Listen to two people talking about sports they play. Write the sports and check (✔) the correct box for each item.

スポーツについて2人が話しているのを聞きましょう。競技名を記入し、それぞれの情報について Yes か No を選びましょう。

1. Sport: _____

	Yes	No
started recently	☐	☐
plays for a club	☐	☐
likes watching it	☐	☐
wants to continue playing	☐	☐

2. Sport: _____

	Yes	No
started recently	☐	☐
plays for a club	☐	☐
likes watching it	☐	☐
wants to continue playing	☐	☐

III ‖Conversation

 60

● **Part 1-1 (Get the gist):** Listen to the conversation and choose the correct answers (a~d).

会話を聞いて、最も適切なものを a ～ d の中から選びましょう。

1. What are Shimpei and Sally mainly talking about?
   a. Sally's teammates
   b. Sally's club
   c. Sports they like
   d. Shimpei's friend

2. How does Shimpei feel about teammates?
   a. He likes them.
   b. He wants some.
   c. He doesn't like them.
   d. He doesn't want any.

● **Part 1-2 (Get the details):** Listen to the conversation again and choose the correct answers (a~d).

もう一度会話を聞いて、最も適切なものを a ～ d の中から選びましょう。

3. Who was Sally talking to before?
   a. Her teammates
   b. Shimpei
   c. Shimpei's friend
   d. Herself

4. What sport does Shimpei play now?
   a. Basketball
   b. Table tennis
   c. Badminton
   d. Bouldering

5. What does Sally recommend that Shimpei do?
   a. Try bouldering
   b. Go to the gym
   c. Do things by himself
   d. Think of his friend as a
      teammate

● **Part 2:** Listen to the conversation again and write the missing words or phrases in the spaces.

会話をもう一度聞いて、空欄に適語を書き入れましょう。

Shimpei: Who were you just (1) _____ _____, Sally? I don't know them.

Sally: They're my teammates from my basketball club, Shimpei. Why?

Shimpei: They looked very (2) _____ and it looked like you were having fun.

Sally: Yes, they're great. I love basketball, but I love them more! We have a match tomorrow. Do you play any sports?

Shimpei: Yes, I do. I'd like some teammates, but I prefer individual sports. I (3) _____ _____ _____ table tennis, but now I play badminton. I have a tournament soon. I'm going to try bouldering, too, something that doesn't need a racket!

Sally: What's bouldering? I've never (4) _____ of it.

Shimpei: It's like rock climbing, but people do it (5) _____ and it's done on a smaller wall.

Sally: Sounds like fun. I think I've seen a gym with a wall like that before.

Shimpei: Yes, it's (6) _____ _____ _____. My friend does it and is a coach. He invited me to try it with him.

Sally: So, you don't just do things by (7) _____. You should think of him as your teammate!

● **Speaking Practice:** Practice the conversation with your partner.

パートナーと一緒に会話を練習しましょう。

IV Pronunciation Check

規則動詞　-ed の発音

動詞を過去形にするとき、後ろに -d または -ed を付けて変化させるものがあります。これらを規則動詞と呼びます。スペルは -d / -ed で同じでも単語によって発音が異なる場合があるので、注意する必要があります。例えば、move の過去形は moved で、語尾を【d】の形で発音します。start の過去形は started で、語尾は【ɪd】の形になります。しかし、look の過去形 looked の発音は【lʊkt】で、語尾が濁らない【t】の音です。これら 3 種類の発音を覚えておきましょう。

Exercises

 61

● **Listen to the recording and choose the correct pronunciation for the underlined words in the sentences below. Then, practice saying the sentences, paying attention to the sounds /d/, /ɪd/ and /t/.**

音声を聞いて、下線の引いてある語の正しい発音を選びましょう。答えを確認し、【d】, 【ɪd】, 【t】に気をつけながら発音の練習をしましょう。

1. When I <u>visited</u> Munich, my friend <u>cooked</u> me a special meal.

   visited　a. /d/ b. /ɪd/ c. /t/　cooked　a. /d/ b. /ɪd/ c. /t/

2. The door of the classroom <u>opened</u>, and the students <u>walked</u> out chatting.

   opened　a. /d/ b. /ɪd/ c. /t/　walked　a. /d/ b. /ɪd/ c. /t/

3. After Ron <u>finished</u> his homework, he <u>tried</u> to make dinner.

   finished　a. /d/ b. /ɪd/ c. /t/　tried　a. /d/ b. /ɪd/ c. /t/

V Focus on Function

used to . . .　の使い方

動詞の use「使う」の過去形・過去分詞の used は、助動詞として "used to . . ." の形で過去の習慣を示す「よく〜したものだ」、または過去の状態を示す「以前は〜だった」という意味で使われます。to の後ろには動詞の原形が続きます。この場合、過去形・過去分詞の used【juːzd】と違い、発音が【juːst】となるので注意しましょう。

例）He used to go to the park when he was a child.
　　（子供の頃、彼はよくその公園に行っていました）
　　I used to play table tennis, but now I play badminton.
　　（以前は卓球をしていましたが、今はバドミントンをします）

Exercises

● **Choose the correct word or phrase for each sentence.**

英文を見て文章に合う語を選びましょう。

1. My father _____ smoke, but he stopped.
   a. used　b. used to　c. was used to
2. Alicia _____ her key to open the door.
   a. used　b. used to　c. was used to
3. We _____ chat about baseball until late at night.
   a. are used　b. used　c. used to

VI │ Find out

● **Find out about your classmates. Ask three people the following questions.**

クラスメートに質問してみましょう。3人に聞いて、答えを書いてください。

	Partner 1	Partner 2	Partner 3
1. How often do you exercise?			
2. Do you prefer individual or team sports?			
3. Do you like to watch sports on TV?			
4. Have you ever watched a game at a stadium?			
5. Are you a member of a sports club?			
6. What's a sport you'd like to try?			
7. Your question: _____?			

Useful Language

Questions

- How often do you . . . ?
- Have you ever watched . . . ?
- Are you a member of . . . ?

Answers

- I play . . .
- Yes, I have. / No, I haven't.
- I'm in . . . / I'm a member of . . .

Details

- Sports: basketball / tennis / golf / soccer / boxing / wrestling / American football / rugby / swimming / badminton / skiing / triathlon

Notes

部活やクラブに入っているというときは、"I'm in the tennis club." のように、in を使って表現します。または、"I'm a member of the tennis club." と、そのクラブの一員であることを示す言い方もあります。"team" の時は、アメリカ英語では "I'm on the team."、イギリス英語では "I'm in the team." と言う場合があります。

UNIT
13

Where are you going?
– Talking about Travel and Vacations

I Vocabulary

● **Part 1:** Match the Japanese words (a~j) to the English words and phrases (1~10).
1～10 の語の意味として適切なものを a～j から選びましょう。

a. ウィンタースポーツ	b. 涼しい	c. 経験	d. 添乗員	e. 冒険
f. 浜辺	g. 小冊子	h. 潜水	i. 国	j. 海外へ

1. ____ beach
2. ____ adventure
3. ____ cool
4. ____ diving
5. ____ winter sports
6. ____ abroad
7. ____ country
8. ____ tour guide
9. ____ brochure
10. ____ experience

● **Part 2:** Complete the dialogs with words and phrases from Part 1.
Part 1 の単語リストから適切な語を選んで文を完成させましょう。

1. **A:** What do you want to do this vacation?
   B: I want to go to Niigata and do some _____, especially snowboarding.

2. **A:** How many times have you been _____?
   B: Three. I've been to the UK, Malaysia, and Korea.

3. **A:** I really want to try _____, but I'm a bit scared.
   B: Me, too. Being under water for a very long time does seem scary.

4. **A:** How was your trip?
   B: It was great. Our _____ was really friendly and we learned a lot.

5. **A:** What's a(n) _____ you'd like to visit?
   B: India. The culture is very different from here. I'd like to experience it for myself.

Listening Practice 1: Listen to the conversation and check (✔) the boxes next to the sentences you hear.

会話を聞いて、どちらの表現が使われているか選んでチェックを入れましょう。

Speaker A	Speaker B
☐ What are your plans for this vacation? ☐ What are you doing this vacation?	
	☐ I'm going to Bangkok with two friends. ☐ I'm not sure, but I want to go to Bangkok.
Why Bangkok?	☐ I want to try real Thai food. ☐ I want to go to a kickboxing match there.
☐ Can you speak Thai? ☐ Have you learned any Thai?	
	No, but lots of people there can speak English or Japanese.
☐ How long do you want to go for? ☐ How long are you going for?	
	I want to go for two weeks, but I only have eight days vacation.
☐ That's still a long time. Have fun! ☐ That's a shame. Have fun anyway.	
	☐ Thanks, I will. ☐ Thank you, I'm sure I will.

Speaking Practice: Practice the conversation with your partner.

パートナーと会話を練習しましょう。

🎧 63, 64

Listening Practice 2: Listen to two people talking about places they visited. Write the places and check (✔) the correct box for each item.

2人が訪れたことのある場所について話しているのを聞きましょう。場所を記入し、それぞれの情報について Yes か No を選びましょう。

1. Place: _____

	Yes	No
went with friends	☐	☐
stayed in a hotel	☐	☐
went to the beach	☐	☐
wants to go back	☐	☐

2. Place: _____

	Yes	No
went with friends	☐	☐
stayed in a hotel	☐	☐
went to the beach	☐	☐
wants to go back	☐	☐

III ‖Conversation 65

● **Part 1-1 (Get the gist):** Listen to the conversation and choose the correct answers (a~d).

会話を聞いて、最も適切なものを a ～ d の中から選びましょう。

1. Which of the following is probably true?
   a. Tipi has been to more countries than Jun.
   b. Jun is a tour guide.
   c. Tipi and Jun will travel together.
   d. Jun likes to visit hot countries.

2. Which country are they most likely in?
   a. Japan
   b. Greece
   c. Canada
   d. Finland

● **Part 1-2 (Get the details):** Listen to the conversation again and choose the correct answers (a~d).

もう一度会話を聞いて、最も適切なものを a ～ d の中から選びましょう。

3. Where could Jun ride a camel?
   a. Greece
   b. Egypt
   c. Canada
   d. Finland

4. Where would Jun prefer to visit?
   a. Europe
   b. A cool place
   c. A hot place
   d. A non-English-speaking country

5. What does Jun say he wants to do?
   a. To have a new experience
   b. To eat great food
   c. To go to a beautiful beach
   d. To see the Pyramids

● **Part 2:** Listen to the conversation again and write the missing words or phrases in the spaces.

会話をもう一度聞いて、空欄に適語を書き入れましょう。

Tipi: Hi, Jun. What are you reading?

Jun: It's a travel brochure, Tipi. I'm looking for (1) _____ to visit this vacation.

Tipi: Do you have any ideas? Maybe I (2) _____ _____ _____ decide.

Jun: Well, I've never been abroad, so I want to go to a place that's very (3) _____ from Japan. I want a new experience.

Tipi: How about Greece? The food is great, there are beautiful (4) _____, and it was really relaxing when I went there, too.

Jun: (5) _____ _____ _____, but I'm not so interested in Europe . . .

Tipi: OK, why not visit Egypt? You could see the Pyramids and ride a camel.

Jun: That would be great, but I prefer cool places. Egypt would be too hot.

Tipi: Oh. Then (6) _____ _____ _____ to Canada or my country, Finland. You might be able to do some winter sports or even see the aurora if you're lucky.

Jun: That would be amazing. I want to go to an English-speaking country, so Canada is (7) _____ best.

● **Speaking Practice:** Practice the conversation with your partner.

パートナーと一緒に会話を練習しましょう。

IV Pronunciation Check

cool と could : 「ウ」の発音

英語の /u/ と /ʊ/ の発音は、カタカナで表そうとするとどちらも「ウ」になりますが、これらには違いがあります。形容詞 cool は【kuːl】と発音し、【uː】の音を出しながら口をすぼめます。多くの単語がこの音を伸ばす形で発音します。can の過去形 could は【kʊd】と発音し、【ʊ】は口を強くすぼめません。発音の違いに注意して、練習してみましょう。

例）You could see the temple. 【kʊd】
　　I prefer cool places. 　　【kuːl】

Exercises

 66

● Listen to the recording and circle the sounds that are used in the underlined words. Then, practice saying the sentences, paying attention to the sounds /uː/ and /ʊ/.

音声を聞いて、下線部の語の発音として聞こえたほうを丸で囲みましょう。その後、正しい発音をチェックし、【uː】と【ʊ】に気をつけながら発音の練習をしましょう。

	woman	move
1. The woman had to move her car.	a. /uː/ b. /ʊ/	a. /uː/ b. /ʊ/

	blue	woods
2. A blue bird was seen in the woods.	a. /uː/ b. /ʊ/	a. /uː/ b. /ʊ/

	foot	pool
3. Lionel injured his foot at the side of the pool.	a. /uː/ b. /ʊ/	a. /uː/ b. /ʊ/

V Focus on Function

could の使い方

助動詞 could は can の過去形として「〜できた」、「〜することが可能だった」という意味で使いますが、その他に現在または未来に関する可能性や推量を表す場合があります。確信の度合いは may や might よりも低いものです。
例）It could be true.（それは本当かもしれない）
また、丁寧な提案を示すときにも使います。
例）Could you tell me where the bank is?（銀行はどこか教えていただけますか？）
Can you . . . ? よりも丁寧な言い方です。

Exercises

● Choose the correct word for each sentence.

次の英文を読み、正しい語を選びましょう。

1. I (**can / could**) play the violin very well, if I practiced long and hard.
2. When I was a child, I (**can't / couldn't**) play tennis. But I (**can / could**) play it now.
3. I wish I (**can / could**) go with you, but I (**can't / couldn't**).

77

VI | Find out

● **Find out about your classmates. Ask three people the following questions.**

クラスメートに質問してみましょう。3人に聞いて、答えを書いてください。

	Partner 1	Partner 2	Partner 3
1.What did you do in your last vacation?			
2. What's the best trip you've ever been on?			
3. Would you prefer to travel alone or in a group?			
4. Have you ever been abroad?			
5. What's a country you'd like to visit?			
6. What's the most beautiful place you've ever been to?			
7. Your question: _____?			

Useful Language

Questions

- What did you do . . . ?
- Have you ever been to . . . ?
- What's the best . . . ?

Answers

- I enjoyed . . .
- Yes, I have. / No, I haven't.
- I think . . . is the best . . .

Details

- Activities: fishing / hiking / climbing / water sports / winter sports / dancing / diving
- Places: seaside / mountain / river / countryside / shopping mall / museum / castle

Notes

「〜に行ったことがある」は、経験を表す現在完了の have (has) been to . . . を使います。have (has) gone to . . . は「〜に行って今はここにいない」という意味になるので、違いに注意しましょう。

UNIT 14

Do you work?
– Talking about Work and Jobs

I ‖ Vocabulary

● **Part 1:** Match the Japanese words (a~j) to the English words and phrases (1~10).
1 ～ 10 の語の意味として適切なものを a ～ j から選びましょう。

a. くつろぐ	b. 面接	c. 夜更かしをする	d. 残業	e. 経歴
f. 仕事	g. 退職する	h. 同僚	i. アルバイトの	j. 給料

1. _____ part-time   2. _____ job   3. _____ relax
4. _____ career   5. _____ overtime   6. _____ salary
7. _____ stay up   8. _____ retire   9. _____ interview
10. _____ colleague

● **Part 2:** Complete the dialogs with words and phrases from Part 1.
Part 1 の単語リストから適切な語を選んで文を完成させましょう。

1. **A:** Do you have a(n) _____?
   B: Yes, I work at a convenience store.

2. **A:** Do you enjoy your work?
   B: Yes, but the _____ is so low. I wish I got paid more.

3. **A:** What's the best thing about your job?
   B: It's my _____. They're all really helpful and friendly.

4. **A:** What's wrong, Jenna?
   B: I've got a(n) _____ for a new job. I'm really nervous.

5. **A:** You look tired.
   B: I really am. I just finished doing some _____ at work. It was so hard!

● **Listening Practice 1:** Listen to the conversation and check (✔) the boxes next to the sentences you hear.

会話を聞いて、どちらの表現が使われているか選んでチェックを入れましょう。

Speaker A	Speaker B
☐ Nice shirt, Hiro!	
☐ Why are you wearing a shirt, Hiro?	
	I'm wearing it for an interview. ☐
	I'm going to an interview. ☐
☐ An interview? What for?	
	A new job at a cram school. ☐
	To start working at a cram school. ☐
☐ A cram school? Where?	
☐ A cram school? What's that?	
	In Japanese it's *juku*. ☐
	It's in Harajuku. ☐
☐ What are you going to teach?	
	If I get the job, I'll teach English. ☐
	I want to teach English. ☐
☐ Wow! Good luck!	
☐ Wow! Try your best!	
	Thanks, I will! ☐
	Thanks! ☐

● **Speaking Practice:** Practice the conversation with your partner.

パートナーと会話を練習しましょう。

🎵 68, 69

● **Listening Practice 2:** Listen to two people talking about their jobs. Write the jobs and check (✔) the correct box for each item.

仕事について2人が話しているのを聞きましょう。職種を記入し、それぞれの情報について Yes か No を選びましょう。

1. Job: _____

	Yes	No
works part-time	☐	☐
finds it interesting	☐	☐
likes their colleagues	☐	☐
wants to stay	☐	☐

2. Job: _____

	Yes	No
works part-time	☐	☐
finds it interesting	☐	☐
likes their colleagues	☐	☐
wants to stay	☐	☐

III ‖ Conversation

 70

● **Part 1-1 (Get the gist):** Listen to the conversation and choose the correct answers (a~d).

会話を聞いて、最も適切なものを a～d の中から選びましょう。

1. What can we infer about Kota?
   a. He writes books.
   b. He works full-time.
   c. He is a student.
   d. He is a teacher.

2. Where are they most likely?
   a. At university
   b. At a restaurant
   c. At a bookstore
   d. At a bank

● **Part 1-2 (Get the details):** Listen to the conversation again and choose the correct answers (a~d).

もう一度会話を聞いて、最も適切なものを a～d の中から選びましょう。

3. Where does Kota work?
   a. At a family restaurant and a bookstore
   b. At a bookstore and a university
   c. At a family restaurant and a university
   d. At a family restaurant, a bookstore, and a university

4. What didn't Alice know?
   a. Kota was tired.
   b. Kota has a job.
   c. Kota often stays up late.
   d. Kota has time to relax.

5. Why does Alice say Kota should be careful?
   a. Because he stays up late.
   b. Because he needs to relax sometimes.
   c. Because he eats a lot of food.
   d. Because he reads a lot.

Part 2: Listen to the conversation again and write the missing words or phrases in the spaces.

会話をもう一度聞いて、空欄に適語を書き入れましょう。

Alice: Hi, Kota. Are you okay? (1) _____ _____

_____. Was that your last class?

Kota: Hi, Alice. Yes, I am tired, and it was my last class. I still need to go to work, though.

Alice: I didn't know you have a job. Where do you (2) _____?

Kota: I don't have one job, I have two! I work at a family restaurant and a

(3) _____.

Alice: No wonder you're so tired. I don't think I could do that. When do you

(4) _____ _____ _____ your university studies?

Kota: It's (5) _____ to find time, so I stay up late a lot. That's why I'm tired!

Alice: You should be careful. Remember, having time to relax is important, too.

Kota: I know, but I (6) _____ _____ _____.
I don't see them as careers, but I get paid a lot for doing overtime and I can get free food at the restaurant and read books for free at the bookstore.

Alice: So, you can make money and (7) _____ money at the same time!

Kota: Exactly!

Speaking Practice: Practice the conversation with your partner.

パートナーと一緒に会話を練習しましょう。

IV Pronunciation Check

work と walk の発音

日本人が間違いやすい発音の一つが work【wɜːk】と walk【wɔːk】です。前者は口をそれほど大きく開けず、後者の方が口を縦に開けて、こもらない音になります。war「戦争」の発音は【wɔːr】で、こちらも間違いやすいので気をつけましょう。リスニングで正しい発音を何度も聞き、実際に声に出して練習し、身につけていくことが大切です。

例) I work at the station.
　　 I walk to the station.

Exercises

● **Listen to the recording and circle the words you hear in the sentences below. Then, practice saying the sentences, paying attention to the sounds /ɜː/ and /ɔː/.**
音声を聞いて、聞こえたほうを丸で囲みましょう。その後、正しい発音をチェックし、【ɜː】と【ɔː】に気をつけながら発音を練習してみましょう。

1. She got (**bird / bored**) when she went (**bird- / board-**) watching.

2. I hope (**walls / worlds**) separating people are removed all over the (**wall / world**).

3. (**Warms / Worms**) become active in spring because the weather gets (**worm / warm**).

V Focus on Function

That's why . . . 「だから、〜なのです。」

何かの理由を先に示して、その結果や結論を表現するときには、関係副詞 why を使って、That's why . . . の形で表すことができます。「だから、〜なのです」、「そういうわけで〜なのです」という意味になります。後ろには主語・動詞と文章が続くので覚えておきましょう。本来は「That's the reason why S + V」の形ですが、the reason が省略されて使われることが多いです。

例 1) My teacher gave us a lot of homework. That's why I'm tired today!
例 2) A: My teacher gave us a lot of homework.
　　　 B: That's why you're tired today!

Exercises

● **Look at the sentences below and write a reply using the specified words and _That's why_.**
カッコの中の語を使って、会話の続きを That's why で表現してみましょう。

1. A: Lora has lived in Spain for three years. (speak, Spanish)
   B: _____

2. A: I got caught up in a traffic jam. (late, work)
   B: _____

3. A: He is a member of the water polo club. (good at, swimming)
   B: _____

VI Find out

● **Find out about your classmates. Ask three people the following questions.**

クラスメートに質問してみましょう。3人に聞いて、答えを書いてください。

	Partner 1	Partner 2	Partner 3
1. Do you have a part-time job?			
2. What's a job you'd like to do?			
3. What's a job you'd never do?			
4. What jobs do your parents do?			
5. Which is more important, good colleagues or a good salary?			
6. At what age do you want to retire?			
7. Your question: _____?			

Useful Language

Questions

- Do you have . . . ?
- What's a job . . . ?
- At what age do you want to . . . ?

Answers

- Yes, I do. / No, I don't.
- I'd like to . . .
- At . . . years old, I want to . . .

Details

- Occupations: doctor / artist / chef / lawyer / farmer / conductor / nurse / bank clerk / tour guide / engineer / journalist / receptionist / store clerk

Notes

「アルバイトをする」は、"do a part-time job" または "work part-time" と表現します。日本語のアルバイトは、ドイツ語の Arbeit に由来する言葉で、英語ではないので気をつけましょう。

UNIT 15

What do you want to do?
– Talking about Plans

I Vocabulary

● **Part 1:** Match the Japanese words (a~j) to the English words and phrases (1~10).
1 ～ 10 の語の意味として適切なものを a ～ j から選びましょう。

| a. 祝日 | b. 考え | c. 自由な | d. 混みあった | e. 計画 |
| f. 祝う | g. テーマパーク | h. 退屈な | i. 自由時間 | j. 一人で |

1. ＿＿＿ crowded   2. ＿＿＿ boring   3. ＿＿＿ plan（名）
4. ＿＿＿ idea   5. ＿＿＿ national holiday   6. ＿＿＿ free time
7. ＿＿＿ [be] free   8. ＿＿＿ theme park   9. ＿＿＿ by yourself
10. ＿＿＿ celebrate

● **Part 2:** Complete the dialogs with words and phrases from Part 1.
Part 1 の単語リストから適切な語を選んで文を完成させましょう。

1. **A:** Do you like Tokyo Disneyland?
   B: Yes, I do. But my favorite ＿＿＿＿＿＿＿＿ is USJ.

2. **A:** Our next lesson is Mr. Tanaka's history class.
   B: Oh no. His lessons are so ＿＿＿＿＿＿＿＿. I always fall asleep.

3. **A:** Why don't we meet at the statue of Hachiko in Shibuya?
   B: How about a different place? Lots of people meet there, so it's always
   ＿＿＿＿＿＿＿＿.

4. **A:** What are you going to do in the summer vacation?
   B: I'm not sure. I haven't made any ＿＿＿＿＿＿＿＿ yet.

5. **A:** I live with my mother, father, four brothers, two sisters, and six dogs.
   B: Wow! You must really look forward to spending time ＿＿＿＿＿＿＿＿.

● Listening Practice 1: Listen to the conversation and check (✔) the boxes next to the sentences you hear.

会話を聞いて、どちらの表現が使われているか選んでチェックを入れましょう。

Speaker A	Speaker B
☐ Are you free tomorrow? ☐ Are you busy on Saturday?	
	☐ Yes, I am. Why? ☐ No, I'm not. Why?
☐ Shall we do something together? ☐ Let's do something together.	
	Sure. What do you want to do?
☐ How about going shopping? ☐ What about going to the beach?	
	☐ That sounds great. Where shall we meet? ☐ Nice idea. I need to buy a new dress.
Why don't we meet at the station?	
	☐ At the station? What time? ☐ All right. What time should I come?
☐ Let's meet at one o'clock. ☐ How about two thirty?	
	☐ Okay. It's a date. ☐ That's fine with me. See you then.

● Speaking Practice: Practice the conversation with your partner.

パートナーと会話を練習しましょう。

CD 73, 74

● Listening Practice 2: Listen to two people talk about their plans. Write when they are talking about and check (✔) the correct box for each item.

2人の人物がある予定について話しているのを聞きましょう。いつの予定なのか記入し、それぞれの情報について Yes か No を選びましょう。

1. When: _____

	Yes	No
staying at home	☐	☐
going shopping	☐	☐
watching a movie	☐	☐
exercising	☐	☐

2. When: _____

	Yes	No
staying at home	☐	☐
going shopping	☐	☐
watching a movie	☐	☐
exercising	☐	☐

III ||Conversation

 75

● **Part 1-1 (Get the gist):** Listen to the conversation and choose the correct answers (a~d).

会話を聞いて、最も適切なものを a ～ d の中から選びましょう。

1. Why are Alex and Minori making plans?
    a. Because tomorrow is Minori's birthday.
    b. Because tomorrow is a national holiday.
    c. Because they are a little bored.
    d. Because they want to do something fun.

2. What will they probably <u>not</u> do tomorrow?
    a. Go to work
    b. Go to a theme park
    c. Go to karaoke
    d. Meet Nanami

● **Part 1-2 (Get the details):** Listen to the conversation again and choose the correct answers (a~d).

もう一度会話を聞いて、最も適切なものを a ～ d の中から選びましょう。

3. How does Alex feel about theme parks?
    a. He thinks they are fun.
    b. He prefers to play computer games.
    c. He likes shopping better.
    d. He doesn't like them.

4. What did Alex remember?
    a. Nanami likes shopping.
    b. Minori likes Disney.
    c. It is Nanami's birthday soon.
    d. Minori likes singing.

5. What does Nanami like?
    a. Computer games
    b. Shopping
    c. Disney
    d. Theme parks

● **Part 2:** Listen to the conversation again and write the missing words or phrases in the spaces.

会話をもう一度聞いて、空欄に適語を書き入れましょう。

Alex: Tomorrow is a national holiday. What are you (1) _____ _____ _____, Minori?

Minori: Hi, Alex. I don't have any plans for tomorrow. Maybe I'll just stay home and relax. I (2) _____ a new computer game last week and I want to play it some more.

Alex: Just playing a computer game by yourself sounds a little boring. Do (3) _____ _____ _____ _____ something together?

Minori: Okay. What do you want to do? How about going clothes shopping? Or maybe we could go to karaoke?

Alex: Definitely not shopping! What about something more (4)_____? Why don't we go to a theme park? Riding a roller coaster is great fun.

Minori: I'm not sure, theme parks are really (5) _____ on national holidays.

Alex: Wait a moment. I've just remembered that tomorrow is Nanami's birthday!

Minori: You're right. She loves Disney, doesn't she? We should go to Tokyo Disneyland and (6) _____ her birthday there.

Alex: That's a good idea. But, she loves singing, too. What should we do?

Minori: Why don't we do both? Let's go to Tokyo Disneyland first, and then go to karaoke. I'll call Nanami and (7) _____ _____ _____.

● **Speaking Practice:** Practice the conversation with your partner.

パートナーと一緒に会話を練習しましょう。

IV Pronunciation Check

消える音／g

Unit 9 では、副詞の前にある t の音が消えるリダクションについて学びました。今回は、語尾にくる g の音が消えるリダクションを覚えましょう。単語が -ing などで終わる場合、最後の g はあいまいに発音し、聞こえないことがあります。また、くだけた言い方として最後の g をアポストロフィで省略した表記をすることもあります。

例）coming → comin'［最後の g を省略した表記］

Exercises

 76

● **Listen to the recording and circle the word which is reduced. Then, practice saying the sentences, paying attention to reduction.**
音声を聞いて、リダクションが起きている語に印を付けましょう。その後、リダクションに注意しながら発音を練習してみましょう。

1. I'm **going shopping** to buy a new **bag** with my friend tomorrow.
   a. going   b. shopping   c. bag
2. Katie and Dave are **going** to a Greek restaurant after **watching** the **skiing** on TV.
   a. going   b. watching   c. skiing
3. The **big** house doesn't **belong** to Mr. Carter. It has **nothing** to do with him.
   a. big   b. belong   c. nothing

V Focus on Function

Why don't you . . . ?「～してみたら？」

相手に何か提案をしたいとき、Why don't you . . . ? を使って「～してはみてはどう？」と表現することができます。自分も含めて何かを一緒にしたいとき、勧誘するときは、Why don't we . . . ? という形になります。カジュアルな言い方なので、目上の人には使わないように気をつけましょう。

例）Why don't you get some sleep?（少し眠ったらどう？）
　　Why don't we do it together?（一緒にしてみようよ）

Exercises

● **Translate the Japanese sentences below into English using *why don't*.**
日本文に合うように、空欄に適切な語を入れましょう。

1. スキューバダイビングをしてみたら？　楽しいよ。

   _____ _____ _____ _____ scuba diving? It's fun!

2. 明日の夜、食事でもどうかな？

   _____ _____ _____ have _____ tomorrow night?

3. サラの誕生日会に来ない？

   _____ _____ _____ _____ to Sara's birthday party?

VI Find out

● **Find out about your classmates. Ask three people the following questions.**

クラスメートに質問してみましょう。3人に聞いて、答えを書いてください。

	Partner 1	Partner 2	Partner 3
1. What do you want to do tomorrow?			
2. How will you spend your weekend?			
3. What do you like to do in your free time?			
4. What is a place you would like to visit?			
5. What is an activity you would like to do?			
6. What do you do when you are bored?			
7. Your question: _____?			

Useful Language

Questions
- What do you want to . . . ?
- How will you spend . . . ?
- What is . . . ?

Answers
- I want to . . .
- I will . . .
- I'd like to . . .

Details
- Activities: camping / trekking / having a barbecue / wind surfing / handicrafts / volunteer / drawing / yoga / whale watching / flower arranging / go to a theme park / relax / celebrate / [be] free / [be] by yourself

Notes

動詞の spend は、「(お金などを) 使う」という意味の他に、「(時を) 過ごす、使う」という意味があります。I'll spend the weekend in Spain with my friend.（週末は友人とスペインで過ごします）のように使います。

Appendix

Further Practice for Speaking and Writing

Nice to meet you. – Talking about Ourselves

Interview your classmates. Speak to at least two people.

クラスメートにインタビューしましょう。 少なくとも2人に話しかけてください。

- What's your full name?
- What does your name mean?
- Do you have a nickname?
- Where were you born?
- Where did you grow up?
- Where do you live now?
- Who do you live with now?
- How many people are there in your family?
- What do you do in your free time?
- What's your favorite food?
- Your question: _____
- Your question: _____

What do you think?

Choose one of the statements below. Prepare a short response giving your opinion.

以下のステートメントのいずれかを選択してください。それについてのあなたの考えを短く書いてみましょう。

- Meeting new people is fun.
- We should try to meet people from many different places.

_____

_____

_____

_____

_____

What do you like to do? – Talking about Hobbies and Pastimes

Interview your classmates. Speak to at least two people.

クラスメートにインタビューしましょう。少なくとも２人に話しかけてください。

- What is your hobby or pastime?
- How often do you do your hobby or pastime?
- How much time do you spend doing your hobby or pastime?
- Who do you do your hobby or pastime with?
- Is your hobby or pastime a good way of making friends?
- Do you prefer doing things alone or with other people?
- Do you think you will continue to do your hobby or pastime in the future?
- Why do some people like dangerous hobbies and pastimes?
- Which hobbies or pastimes do you think are the most difficult?
- Do you think people spend too much money on their hobbies and pastimes?
- Your question: _____
- Your question: _____

What do you think?

Choose one of the statements below. Prepare a short response giving your opinion.

以下のステートメントのいずれかを選択してください。それについてのあなたの考えを短く書いてみましょう。

- A hobby or pastime should be exciting.
- People should have more than one hobby or pastime.

_____

_____

_____

_____

_____

Unit 3:

Where are you from? – Talking about Hometowns

Interview your classmates. Speak to at least two people.

クラスメートにインタビューしましょう。少なくとも２人に話しかけてください。

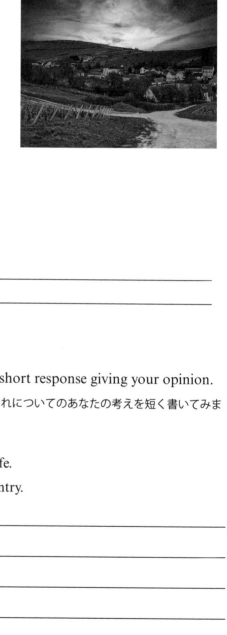

- Where are you from?
- Do you like your hometown?
- What is a good place to visit near your hometown?
- Where do you live now?
- How long have you lived there?
- Do you live in a house or an apartment?
- Do you like where you live?
- Have you ever moved?
- Where would you like to live in the future?
- Would you like to live in a different country?
- Your question: _____
- Your question: _____

What do you think?

Choose one of the statements below. Prepare a short response giving your opinion.

以下のステートメントのいずれかを選択してください。それについてのあなたの考えを短く書いてみましょう。

- I want to live in my hometown all my life.
- People should try living in another country.

_____

_____

_____

_____

_____

Who's that? – Talking about Family

Interview your classmates. Speak to at least two people.

クラスメートにインタビューしましょう。少なくとも２人に話しかけてください。

- Is your family big or small?
- How many people are there in your family?
- Do you have any brothers or sisters?
- Do you have any aunts or uncles?
- Do you have any pets?
- Do you live with your family?
- How often do you see your family?
- When will you next see your family?
- What do you like to do with your family?
- How did your parents meet?
- Your question: _____
- Your question: _____

What do you think?

Choose one of the statements below. Prepare a short response giving your opinion.

以下のステートメントのいずれかを選択してください。それについてのあなたの考えを短く書いてみましょう。

- I never want to have children.
- Bigger families are better than smaller families.

_____

_____

_____

_____

_____

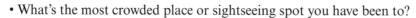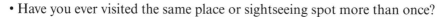

Unit 5:

Where's that? – Talking about Places and Sights

Interview your classmates. Speak to at least two people.

クラスメートにインタビューしましょう。少なくとも２人に話しかけてください。

- What is the most beautiful place you have ever been to?
- Where is a good place to visit in your hometown?
- Where is a place or sightseeing spot that you would like to visit?
- What is the best place or sightseeing spot to visit in your country?
- What's the most crowded place or sightseeing spot you have been to?
- Have you ever visited the same place or sightseeing spot more than once?
- Do you prefer visiting places and sightseeing spots alone or with other people?
- Do you think traveling is too expensive in your country?
- Did you visit any places or sightseeing spots on school trips?
- Do you like to buy souvenirs at the places or sightseeing spots you visit?
- Your question: _____
- Your question: _____

What do you think?

Choose one of the statements below. Prepare a short response giving your opinion.

以下のステートメントのいずれかを選択してください。それについてのあなたの考えを短く書いてみましょう。

- Visiting a museum is better than going to the beach.
- People should try and visit as many places and sightseeing spots as they can.

_____

_____

_____

_____

Unit 6:

How do we get there? – Talking about Transport and Directions

Interview your classmates. Speak to at least two people.

クラスメートにインタビューしましょう。少なくとも２人に話しかけてください。

- Do you have a bicycle?
- Which do you like better, walking or cycling?
- How do you come to school?
- How much money do you spend on travel every week?
- Have you ever flown in a plane?
- What's your favorite kind of transportation?
- How often do you take a taxi?
- Do you prefer taking a bus or a train?
- Can you read a map?
- What would you do if you got lost?
- Your question: _____
- Your question: _____

What do you think?

Choose one of the statements below. Prepare a short response giving your opinion.

以下のステートメントのいずれかを選択してください。それについてのあなたの考えを短く書いてみましょう。

- Trains are better than buses.
- People should walk and cycle more.

_____

_____

_____

_____

_____

Are you hungry? – Talking about Food

Interview your classmates. Speak to at least two people.

クラスメートにインタビューしましょう。少なくとも2人に話しかけてください。

- What's your favorite sweet food?
- Do you drink coffee?
- Do you eat fruit every day?
- Can you cook?
- How much does your lunch usually cost?
- Do you like to try new kinds of food?
- Do you prefer fish or meat?
- Do you like fast food?
- Have you ever eaten *inago no tsukudani*（いなごの佃煮）?
- What's a food or drink you don't like?
- Your question: _____
- Your question: _____

What do you think?

Choose one of the statements below. Prepare a short response giving your opinion.

以下のステートメントのいずれかを選択してください。それについてのあなたの考えを短く書いてみましょう。

- We should try different kinds of food.
- Everybody should learn how to cook.

_____

_____

_____

_____

_____

Unit 8:

Let's eat! – Talking about Restaurants and Meals

Interview your classmates. Speak to at least two people.

クラスメートにインタビューしましょう。少なくとも2人に話しかけてください。

- Which do you prefer, eating out or eating at home?
- How often do you eat out?
- When was the last time you ate out?
- Which do you prefer, going to a restaurant or ordering delivery food?
- How often do you order delivery food?
- What's your favorite restaurant?
- Where is your favorite restaurant?
- What do you usually order at your favorite restaurant?
- How much does a meal at your favorite restaurant cost?
- Are you allergic to anything?
- Your question: _____
- Your question: _____

What do you think?

Choose one of the statements below. Prepare a short response giving your opinion.

以下のステートメントのいずれかを選択してください。それについてのあなたの考えを短く書いてみましょう。

- Restaurants are too expensive.
- Delivery food is very convenient.

_____

_____

_____

_____

Unit 9:

What are you watching? – Talking about Movies and TV

Interview your classmates. Speak to at least two people.

クラスメートにインタビューしましょう。少なくとも2人に話しかけてください。

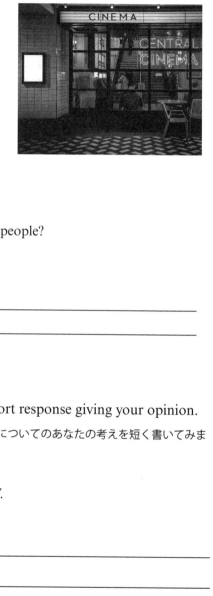

- What's your favorite movie?
- Who is your favorite actor or actress?
- When was the last time you went to the movie theater?
- How often do you rent movies?
- Has a movie ever made you cry?
- Are there any kinds of TV programs that you don't like?
- Who is your favorite TV celebrity?
- Do you prefer to watch TV alone or with other people?
- Do you watch the news on TV?
- Did you watch TV yesterday?
- Your question: _____
- Your question: _____

What do you think?

Choose one of the statements below. Prepare a short response giving your opinion.

以下のステートメントのいずれかを選択してください。それについてのあなたの考えを短く書いてみましょう。

- Reading books is better than watching TV.
- Actors are paid too much money.

_____

_____

_____

_____

_____

Unit 10:

What music do you like? – Talking about Music

Interview your classmates. Speak to at least two people.

クラスメートにインタビューしましょう。少なくとも２人に話しかけてください。

- What kind of music do you like?
- How often do you listen to music?
- Can you play any musical instruments?
- How much time do you spend listening to music?
- Is there any kind of music you hate?
- Have you ever been to a concert?
- Do you like watching music videos?
- Do you like to dance?
- Are you a good singer?
- What is one of your favorite songs?
- Your question: _____
- Your question: _____

What do you think?

Choose one of the statements below. Prepare a short response giving your opinion.

以下のステートメントのいずれかを選択してください。それについてのあなたの考えを短く書いてみましょう。

- Going to live concerts is fun.
- Everyone should learn to play a musical instrument.

_____

_____

_____

_____

_____

Unit 11:

How much is it? – Talking about Shopping

Interview your classmates. Speak to at least two people.

クラスメートにインタビューしましょう。少なくとも2人に話しかけてください。

- Do you like shopping?
- How often do you go shopping?
- Where do you like to shop?
- When did you last go shopping? Where did you go? What did you buy?
- What is the most expensive thing you have ever bought?
- Who do you like going shopping with?
- Do you ever go window shopping?
- Which do you prefer, online shopping or going to a shop?
- What is something you really want to buy?
- What is something you would never buy?
- Your question: _____
- Your question: _____

What do you think?

Choose one of the statements below. Prepare a short response giving your opinion.

以下のステートメントのいずれかを選択してください。それについてのあなたの考えを短く書いてみましょう。

- It is fun to go shopping with friends.
- Online shopping is better than going to a shop.

_____

_____

_____

_____

_____

Unit 12:

Let's play! – Talking about Sports and Exercise

Interview your classmates. Speak to at least two people.

クラスメートにインタビューしましょう。少なくとも2人に話しかけてください。

- Do you play any sports?
- How often do you exercise?
- Do you prefer team sports or individual sports?
- Who is your favorite sportsperson or athlete?
- Would you rather go swimming or skiing?
- Do you think it is okay to gamble on sports events?
- What is your favorite Olympic sport or event?
- Do you like to watch sports on TV?
- Should motor racing be thought of as a sport?
- What's your favorite Japanese martial art?
- Your question: _____
- Your question: _____

What do you think?

Choose one of the statements below. Prepare a short response giving your opinion.

以下のステートメントのいずれかを選択してください。それについてのあなたの考えを短く書いてみましょう。

- Playing sports is the best way to make friends.
- It is better to be healthy and strong than to be intelligent.

_____

_____

_____

_____

_____

Where are you going? – Talking about Travel and Vacations

Interview your classmates. Speak to at least two people.

クラスメートにインタビューしましょう。少なくとも2人に話しかけてください。

- Have you ever been abroad?
- What's the best vacation you've ever had?
- Have you ever got lost while traveling?
- What countries would you like to visit?
- Where in Japan would you like to go to?
- Do you always buy souvenirs when you travel?
- Do you prefer active or relaxing vacations?
- What's the most beautiful place you've ever been to?
- Have you ever been traveling alone?
- Did you go on a school trip in junior high school?
- Your question: _____
- Your question: _____

What do you think?

Choose one of the statements below. Prepare a short response giving your opinion.

以下のステートメントのいずれかを選択してください。それについてのあなたの考えを短く書いてみましょう。

- Traveling somewhere is the best way to learn about a place.
- We should travel in our own country before going abroad.

_____

_____

_____

_____

_____

Unit 14:

Do you work? – Talking about Work and Jobs

Interview your classmates. Speak to at least two people.

クラスメートにインタビューしましょう。少なくとも２人に話しかけてください。

- Do you have a part-time job?
- What kind of work do you want to do in the future?
- What is a job that you wouldn't want to do?
- Have you ever been promoted?
- Would you prefer to work indoors or outdoors?
- Have you ever done any volunteer work?
- What is a good age to retire?
- Would you like to work from home?
- Which is more important, making lots of money or enjoying your job?
- Would you like to work overseas?
- Your question: _____
- Your question: _____

What do you think?

Choose one of the statements below. Prepare a short response giving your opinion.

以下のステートメントのいずれかを選択してください。それについてのあなたの考えを短く書いてみましょう。

- To have one job for your whole life is best.
- Everyone should work abroad for one year.

_____

_____

_____

_____

_____

Unit 15:

What do you want to do? – Talking about Plans

Interview your classmates. Speak to at least two people.

クラスメートにインタビューしましょう。少なくとも2人に話しかけてください。

- What do you want to do tomorrow?
- How will you spend your weekend?
- Do you plan what to do in your free time?
- Are you good at making plans?
- What is a place you would like to visit?
- What is an activity you would like to do?
- What are three things you want to do in your next vacation?
- How much time do you spend planning your vacations?
- How often do you change your plans?
- What are you planning to do after you graduate?
- Your question: _____
- Your question: _____

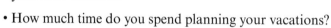

What do you think?

Choose one of the statements below. Prepare a short response giving your opinion.

以下のステートメントのいずれかを選択してください。それについてのあなたの考えを短く書いてみましょう。

- It is good to try lots of new things.
- Making plans is easy.

_____

_____

_____

_____

_____

TEXT PRODUCTION STAFF

edited by	編集
Takashi Kudo	工藤 隆志
Hiromi Oota	太田 裕美

cover design by	表紙デザイン
Nobuyoshi Fujino	藤野 伸芳

CD PRODUCTION STAFF

narrated by	吹き込み者
Josh Keller (AmE)	ジョシュ・ケラー (アメリカ英語)
Karen Haedrich (AmE)	カレン・ヘドリック (アメリカ英語)

Complete Communication Book 1 – Basic –
コミュニケーションのための実践演習Book1〈初級編〉

2022年1月10日　初版印刷
2024年7月30日　第5刷発行

著　　者　James Bury
　　　　　Anthony Sellick
　　　　　堀内 香織
発 行 者　佐野 英一郎
発 行 所　株式会社 成 美 堂
　　　　　〒101-0052　東京都千代田区神田小川町3-22
　　　　　TEL 03-3291-2261　FAX 03-3293-5490
　　　　　https://www.seibido.co.jp

印 刷・製本　萩原印刷株式会社

ISBN 978-4-7919-7241-8　　　　　　　Printed in Japan